Day by Day

Day by Day

The Chronicles of a Hard of Hearing Reporter

Elizabeth Thompson

GALLAUDET UNIVERSITY PRESS
Washington, D.C.

Deaf Lives
A Series Edited by Brenda Brueggemann

Gallaudet University Press
Washington, D.C. 20002
http://gupress.gallaudet.edu

ISBN-13: 978-1-56368-370-1
ISBN-10: 1-56368-370-9

Library of Congress Cataloging-in-Publication Data

Thompson, Elizabeth, 1951–
    Day by day : the chronicles of a hard of hearing reporter / Elizabeth Thompson.
        p. cm.— (Deaf lives)
    ISBN-13: 978-1-56368-391-6 (alk. paper)
    1. Thompson, Elizabeth, 1951–   2. Journalists—United States—Biography.
3. Deaf authors—United States—Biography.   I. Title.
    HV2534.T463 A3 2008
    070.92—dc22
    [B]
                                                                2008007110

Contents

Foreword

I remember one of my first encounters with Liz Thompson. It disappointed me. You see, I was trying to hire Liz to be a reporter for *Suburban News Publications (SNP)*, a group of 21 weekly newspapers in the Columbus (Ohio) metropolitan area. I was the editor and always on the lookout for talent, especially mature professionals with a variety of life experiences. With more than 60 people working on our news staff, many were young reporters and editors gaining their first real journalism, and real life, experience.

But Liz was different. She already had proven herself as a column writer, contributing insightful, slice-of-life pieces regularly as a reader. So when she told me she had an interest in reporting, my welcome door flew wide open. But then Liz had second thoughts—I'm still not sure why—and decided the full-time commitment didn't suit her. So she enlisted as a part-time typist for the copy desk. That was my disappointment; I wanted the full-time reporter version. Still, at least she was in the newsroom, and said perhaps she would try her hand at a free-lance piece, stringer reporting. I still had a shot.

In retrospect, I think Liz's reluctance to report full-time was a matter of self-doubt. She wasn't sure how her deafness would affect her work as a reporter. But Liz has never been one to wallow in the negative. Rather, she's more like the first paratrooper out of the plane. It didn't take long for her to bite on that first assignment and that was that—Liz loved reporting, loved writing, most of all she loved meeting people, talking to them, hearing their stories, and sharing her stories. From there, it was just a matter of waiting until another full-time reporting job opened up. Not surprisingly, that didn't happen quickly, and Liz had to bide her time. Now that she had tasted reporting, however, that waiting game was not easy for her. I got frequent calls reminding me she wanted the next job, asking me if I still was committed to hiring her. That bulldog approach was just one more thing that would make Liz an effective, and extremely prolific, reporter.

The job did finally open up, and Liz did get it. Seldom have I seen a journalist approach his or her job with the enthusiasm, joy really, that Liz mustered virtually every day. If it was a feature story about a senior citizen, Liz was psyched up because that person was such a joy, had such a tale to tell and—invariably—had crossed paths in some way with Liz's experiences. Not only did this give the paper wonderful features, textured with Liz's empathetic style; it also built bridges from our company to the communities in which Liz worked.

And that ebullience wasn't limited to the "good" stories. When government officials stonewalled us on public records or open meetings, Liz revved up to find out what was happening. She would call every official, attend every meeting, and knock on any door necessary to let readers know what was going on. The "hunt" energized her just as much as those conversations with her feature subjects.

Liz wrote a lot of columns about her hearing loss and how it affected her life, but to be honest, it wasn't something I thought about much when I hired her. Why should I have? I talked to her. She talked to me. It didn't seem any different from the communication I had with anyone else.

But the truth is I did get occasional complaints from people that Liz's hearing was a problem. Some of these people were sources. Some were co-workers. Usually, I talked to Liz about them and she would tackle them directly. She would either talk to the concerned party to iron things out, or put herself in a better situation—either through improved technology or physical positioning—to minimize future concerns.

Many of these concerns were not about the communication; they were about the other person's perception of Liz. Because Liz was so open about her hearing loss, they expected the worst. It didn't matter that Liz did excellent work; that fact was obscured for them by what they viewed as an insurmountable handicap.

I saw the same reaction several times with reporters who spoke with an accent. So you learn to consider the source of the complaint, especially when they say, "I'm not prejudiced, but . . ."

That brings us to Liz's super powers. Because of her hearing loss, she said, she had cultivated other senses to "listen." While she could sign and read lips, she was also a master at reading body language. Many was the local politician who told Liz of the unspoken just by the way they handled themselves and her understanding of that.

Liz's energy and enthusiasm not only made her a good reporter, it also made her a great student. She came into the job with an open mind and a huge thirst to learn more. That she did, and she's still at it.

Martin L. Rozenman
Former editor, *Suburban News Publications*
Reporter, *The Columbus Dispatch*

Acknowledgments

All my thanks goes to God who has guided me and sustained me. There is no doubt that God sent every person and circumstance into my life to grant me the strength to persevere.

Some of these people include my husband and best friend, Robert. He listened to my writings over and over through the years and stood by me through everything. Our children, Lisa, Michael and Mary, and her husband Bob, and their children, Jacob, Elizabeth, and Andrew, are a constant source of joy and the breath of fresh air I so often need. My deafness never bothered any of our children. Rather, it probably taught them that parents are far from perfect. Certainly, my children have been subjects of my writing over the years.

As a columnist, then reporter, I should acknowledge the support of Martin Rozenman and Cliff Wiltshire of *Suburban News Publications (SNP)*. Also at *SNP*, I acknowledge Dorothy Stoyer, Ginny Tsai, Mary Mattison, Lisa Proctor, Richard Ades, Anne Maher, Dennis Laycock, Carolyn Farnsworth, and Tom Schluep, my signing buddy. When we moved to Phoenix, Arizona, editor Joel Nilsson with *The Arizona Republic* was patient with my prolific personality as a community columnist and published as much content as he could.

To the readers who took time to write to me either via snail mail or e-mail, thank you. One surprising letter from Joan Campbell, an old high school friend, allowed us to reconnect after thirty-plus years.

Donna Schillinger, current editor for *Hearing Health Magazine* and Lorraine Short, former editor, and Barbara Kelley, current editor, for *Hearing Journal Magazine* were patient and taught me well when I began writing for magazines.

As I delved into Deaf culture, I met wonderful people who taught me to "just communicate." Lori Woods, Juanita Schwartz, Kassandra Schrienk, Irene Cohen, Pastor Ed Bergstresser, and all the wonderful people at Holy Cross Lutheran Church for the Deaf, are some names that easily come to mind. There were many more. With their help, I felt accepted and my last fears of deafness melted away.

This book is my way of thanking each person who has graced my life.

Introduction

The short of it—I became deaf.

The long of it—I learned how to cope. This learning process began when I was a child. Was it easy? No. Interesting? Yes. That is the gist of my book. I want to share what I have learned from within myself, from my experiences, and from others. All of these experiences led to my writing a newspaper column, starting in 1998. I have built my book around these columns, explaining how the writing came to life and any afterthoughts that came to me as I retyped individual columns into my book. The columns, all of which appeared in *Suburban News Publications (SNP)*, are scattered throughout the book. Words have a power that can have a long-lasting effect. For this reason, I want my words to encourage all of my readers and let them know they are not alone. I write with the following scripture in mind,

> Do not let any unwholesome talk come out of your mouths, but only what is helpful for building others up according to their needs, that it may benefit those who listen.
>
> —Ephesians 4:29

I gave up my personal search to learn why I had a hearing loss, once I determined there was a reason for my hearing loss. As the years passed and I continued writing my columns, what began as a coping mechanism for me turned into a mission. I wanted to learn, teach, and reach others struggling like I was, and to build a bridge of understanding between hearing and Deaf people.

My philosophy has grown over the years. I believe hindsight is as close to perfect vision as I can come. Certainly many facts are jaded by the distance of memories and by what I wish might have happened in the past. Inaccuracies abound in the retelling, but it reflects how I remember things, including the sights, scents, and emotions.

I love the classic movie, *It's a Wonderful Life*, and watch it every Christmas. As Clarence, wishing for his angel wings, watches George Bailey's life unfold, he imagines how he can help him. George had been selfless most of his life and had even lost hearing in one ear as a child when he saved his brother from drowning. George thinks he is worth more dead than alive. That is when Clarence comes to earth and earns his angel wings by helping George realize the many ways he has made other people's lives better.

Looking back on my life some fifty-odd years later does not offer the advantages of Frank Capra's direction in the movie. I draw on my own memories to give you as accurate and interesting a view as humanly possible. My life is an open book now and I welcome you into my world.

Acknowledging Differences

As I walked up the steep front steps and opened the massive doors, a familiar aroma filled my senses. The fragrance was a mixture of paste, crayons, ink from mimeographed work papers, wood desks, apples, peanut butter, and the lilacs and daffodils on teachers' desks. Even today if I get a whiff of this concoction, I am transported to my school days. Voices echo through hallways of tall ceilings and wood floors. I can still hear the sound of my saddle shoes on the stairs as I ran to my fourth-grade classroom to find my smiling, kind, and beautiful teacher Mrs. McGlish. Flowers inevitably graced her desk as the immense windows let sunlight flood our room.

Emerson Elementary School was only one block from my house, so I could quickly run home for lunch. Some days, I toted a metal lunch box and for a nickel would buy milk in a glass jar with a white, cardboard top. I loved this building—well, I loved school and learning, especially reading. In my memory there is something magical about this place with its vast size, wide stairs, and cloakrooms where we stashed our coats, boots, and lunch boxes. Our desks were our private place where no one, save our teachers, was allowed. We had to keep them neat, and at the teacher's will, she would raise the wood lids and inspect them.

Third grade was one of my most miserable years in school. Mrs. Freeman, my teacher, at Whittier Elementary put me in the corner the first day of school for talking to my friend Dee. She yelled all the more when I tried to explain I was telling Dee we weren't supposed to talk. Unfortunately, my voice carried like a fog horn, so I could never get away with talking in class. This same teacher also criticized me, as we were learning cursive, "Elizabeth, you will never learn to write." I felt so small. That is also the first year I remember telling a bald-faced lie. Mrs. Freeman asked each of us to share the plans we had for the upcoming spring break. My answer truthfully should have been, "Nothing really, just playing." I'll never know what possessed me to say, "Our family is going to New York." As the words slid out of my mouth, my face must have turned bright red. She knew I was lying; I'm still a lousy liar.

In contrast, fourth grade remains one of my favorite school years, albeit one that holds a vague mystery in my mind. My teacher, Mrs. McGlish, was sweet and good. I sat next to Donald, who had the largest box of Crayola crayons I had ever seen in my life. Silver, gold, and all sorts of reds. I knew it was going to be a good year.

A Dark Room

One school day when I was in fourth grade, Mrs. Agnes O'Keefe, the school nurse, took me to another classroom to have my hearing tested. All I remember is going into a dark room. As I sat in the makeshift testing room, I remember a stillness as the nurse placed the headset on my ears. She asked me to raise a hand when I heard a sound. I can still remember looking around the dark room to take it all in. I was chilled and wanted the cardigan sweater my grandmother had knitted for me. For what seemed like hours, I heard nothing. "When will she start?" I wondered; then, finally, I heard a beep, and I raised my hand. After this test, Mrs. O'Keefe said something about telling my teachers and parents that I had a big hearing loss.

I kept waiting for something to happen after that hearing test. Time passed, but nothing drastically changed. I figured I had imagined it all. Somewhere deep inside, I knew I was on my own in dealing with my hearing loss. I became more visual in conversations and read lips and body language to know what was going on without even realizing I was using this as a coping strategy. At home, when banter flew around the room among my two older brothers and younger sister, I remember feeling lost and just smiling while picking up bits and pieces of their conversations. It became a part of my survival tactics.

In elementary school, I did fine because most teachers looked directly at the class when reading or talking. Later, in junior and senior high, my straight As turned to Bs, Cs, and Ds. By the time I was a junior in high school, I had become a champion bluffer with friends and teachers. I didn't realize until years later why I did poorly in classes such as math, in which the teachers turned their backs to the class and wrote on the blackboard. (This was before whiteboards with markers. We used chalk and felt erasers.) I had *no idea* that while they were writing, they were explaining how to solve a problem or giving us additional information. When I talked with math teachers one on one, I understood the content, but in class—poof!—my understanding slid down the drain. In recent years, my friends have confirmed the teaching styles of our school days, and I have the ability to explain my hearing loss in ways they can understand based on our past common experiences. I had better success in other subjects. English was mostly reading and writing, which did not require hearing. Music class was loud and I could feel the beat and notes. I was also able to read the music. I was in many plays in high school and drama was a matter of repeating lines and waiting for cues. Looking for cues came

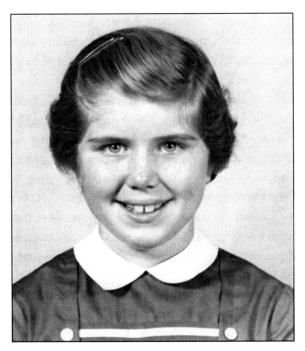

In elementary school, I did fine because most teachers
looked directly at the class when reading or talking.

naturally to me and I memorized entire plays. I convinced myself
that if I knew what was being said, I actually felt I was hearing it. So,
acting in plays was predictable and fun.

Once, my friends Dee (the same Dee from third grade) and Mar-
ilyn went with me to the school counseling office to get our GPAs. I
was too embarrassed to admit that I didn't know what a GPA was.
(I found out later that it means grade point average.) Dee and Mari-
lyn came out discouraged; their averages were lower than expected—
I assumed their GPAs were something like a 3.5 or 3.8 out of 4.0.
When I came out, I could not bring myself to tell them mine was
only 1.8. They smiled and said something like, "You're so smart, you

don't want to brag." Even if they did not say those exact words, it's my memory of how ashamed I felt.

Looking back, I think I could have confided in my friends, but I was unsure of myself. I had known most of my friends since kindergarten. Westerville, Ohio, was a small, friendly village when I was born in 1951. Many of my classmates were highly intelligent and I wondered why they wanted to be friends with me. I felt like quite the dummy who was simply going through the motions.

During this time I was oblivious that many people graced my life with the power to see beyond my exterior and into my heart and soul. Now, I realize Mrs. McGlish was one of those people who seemed to know who I could become. Many adults at our church gave me the same feeling of security she did; they would greet me with open arms and smiles. Even today I can see their faces, and I remember old kindnesses. I will never forget how proud I felt when our neighbors, Ray and Dorothy Schick, gave me my first babysitting job. I was 11 when they asked me to watch their infant grandchild as he slept on a couch. I stood the entire time and earned ten cents for the ten minutes I was with him. Until their deaths many years later, we stayed in touch and enjoyed each others' company.

My visual acuity became sharper as a result of my losing my hearing. While I was reading lips and body language, I noted these many individual differences. Then one day I came across a quote by retired University of Arizona professor Dr. Adela A. Allen. I loved it and often thought about what it meant. I even wrote the following column about it.

Sometimes People Benefit Most from Being Cradled

March 10, 1999

"We should acknowledge differences, we should greet differences, until difference makes no difference anymore." Are these words, by Dr. Adela A. Allen, attainable? I feel confident they are. Maybe I am an eternal optimist, but I believe that at a personal level, this is attainable. One by one, we can make this happen. Thinking on this quote, I realize that many things can set us apart—physically, emotionally and spiritually. Yet we are all on our journeys through life. Sometimes we are myopic and oftentimes our vision is like a wide-angle lens on a camera. Our focus shifts with life's changes. At times, nothing is in focus and life seems a blur.

Many of us struggle with physical limitations. The tangible efforts to walk, talk, see, hear, feel, taste or think don't come easily. Most of us need people in our lives who care enough to at least try to understand or assist us—people who are willing to repeat messages we lost in translation, those who will lend an arm to steady our way, and those true friends who are willing to shed their fears of the unknown and stand beside us through life.

I was listening to a presentation about epilepsy at a community health fair. My main concern has always been, "What do they need me to do if I witness a seizure?" I asked and the response was simple enough: "Cradle their head in your hands so they will not harm themselves, and then call for help." Cradle their head in your hands. Or place their head on your lap and call for help until the seizure passes. Nothing else is required during this crisis time.

How often might we feel that we are having a personal seizure whether physical, emotional or spiritual. If only someone would cradle our head long enough for us to feel safe until the crisis is past. Then we could stand up and say, "Thank you." We would then have the strength and example to follow to help others overcome their crises. And one by one, we would pass this unconditional love to our fellow travelers.

When a person loses her hearing, the world as she knew it is shattered—physically, emotionally and, often, spiritually. How we work and play takes a dramatic turn. Our ability to participate in our world is deeply affected and relationships are altered. A person who cannot hear well may appear to be ignoring you. It would be easy to assume they are rude. You might try again by facing the person. Let them know you are talking with them, smile and repeat your message.

There are choices to make but often we don't know what questions to ask or where to begin. After the crisis—of learning how to cope and accept our loss—passes, we can choose to help someone else. While I was learning sign language, I wanted to do it perfectly and stressed myself to the maximum. It stifled me terribly. When I finally realized that communication was the key, I relaxed. I strived for effective, not perfect, communication.

It is a noisy world. When one wears hearing aids, machines, overhead announcements and other noise makes conversation virtually impossible. A friendly smile may be all it takes to break the barriers to communication. Cradle their emotions. Respect the person.

Another scenario is when a person who uses a wheelchair comes to a doorway too small for them to pass through. What might you do if you saw this happening? You might not know what to do, so you can ask them. Maybe find another route for them or do what a friend of mine did when met with this situation. He basically "cradled their head" by getting assistance and pushing them through the tight entryway. No big deal, just assist and let them move on their way.

Or you see a person stumbling through a store, maybe knocking down a display. What would you do? It might be natural to make incorrect assumptions. They might have stumbled for physical reasons you cannot see, such as multiple sclerosis or poor vision. You could offer assistance by picking up the display and assuring they are not hurt. Smile and move on. The physical aspects of our lives affect our emotions and spirit. All three work in unison. Each time a person displays compassion, our heart is filled with hope. Emotions are stabilized and our spirit is restored.

The movie *Grand Canyon* is about how unique we are. It allows us to see how we travel similar roads through life and sometimes they intersect. Then we meet the differences head on. In the closing scene, the very diverse cast stand at the edge of the Grand Canyon and, with awe, take in the powerful beauty.

One character asks, "Well, what do you think?"
The answer: "I think—it's not all bad."
Is the opening quote attainable? That is for each of us to decide. We may never know when it may be our turn to need a fellow traveler to ease our way.

As I considered my fellow travelers, I didn't realize some were as confused as I was. Robert Frost's poem "The Road Less Traveled" spoke to me and my thoughts became a published column in *SNP*.

We Can Grow Greatly from the Road Less Traveled
July 29, 1998

Robert Frost clearly stated in his poem, 'The Road Less Traveled,' that the road we choose makes "all the difference." I agree. But I have taken so many detours and wasted so much time. I thought I had chosen wisely (that sounds like a scene from *Indiana Jones—The Last Crusade*) only to learn that I had chosen a road riddled with briars, deep valleys, and steep mountains.

Like me, have you spent time holding your head bemoaning the "Why me?" over and over? Life is not easy but with me, I had to be quite a bit older to see why it's not easy. Anything worth its salt is tough and not handed to you on a silver platter. I just wanted a break, but I went around thinking someone else was responsible for providing it. When I woke up, so to speak, I realized my strength does not come from others but from within, by way of God.

Wait, that's right. Maybe I had chosen wisely. In his poem, Frost chose the road on which grass had not been beaten down, a road less traveled. Then why would he or anyone consider this to be the best road to travel? If it were fraught with obstacles and potential hazards, why would we choose that path instead of the one that is open and clear? The open and clear path would be an easy stroll; we could bask in the warm sunlight and walk with ease.

But the overgrown path requires muscle, ingenuity, talents, deep thought, planning, prayer . . . hey, that sounds like life to me, a life with value, learning, growth and deep meaning. It seems that our strengths—physical, emotional and spiritual—would be heightened. Life would be more interesting. The sky would not always be blue. Is it anyway? The rain would fall. The seeds would grow into trees, flowers and vegetables. When the sun shines, we appreciate it more and get out and play. Seems to me that life where obstacles have been hurdled, achievements reached with much effort and an ability to accept our lives—making the most of the sunny days—is the best choice.

In my past, I often wondered why my hearing loss existed. I spent a lot of time at the crossroads trying to start on the open path. My feet never budged. On that path I would have allowed self-pity to take hold and my growth to be stunted. I had to climb my mountain and see the view on the other side. It took me years to climb that mountain. The view was worth the climb. Now I have accepted this loss as part of who I am. Now I have the inner strength to advocate for others and myself.

Yes, I have a significant hearing loss but there is so much more to me. Here is an excerpt from a poem I wrote for a woman who is hard of hearing and legally blind.

> When you look at me, hear me laugh, see me smile . . .
> work a little at getting past, what I may no longer have.
> Please see who I am, tell me a joke, talk to me about your day, let
>   me watch your children play. Tell them, too, that I'm just like
>   them.
> A person, with heart, one of God's loving gems . . . then the
>   bridge will grow and grow
> And the world will be better, the flowers will grow
> They will perk up their blossoms and laugh at the sun,
> All of life will be beauty and we will learn how to show
> True love and true friendship
> To each person we know.

I have been called "brave" to speak and write so openly about my invisible condition, my hearing loss. Many people try to hide something that the world might think of as a deficiency. My condition, and other unseen challenges, is worth owning, accepting. Can you change it? Are you able to make this condition disappear? My hope is to use my life experience and assist others through this time of acceptance.

In American Sign Language, the sign for 'accept' is wonderful. Take your hands and place them, palm down, in front of you with your fingers spread. Now draw your fingers together and pull your hands to your upper chest. Think about it—taking something "out of the air" and placing it on you, accepting it, receiving it to yourself. Saying, in your heart, "Ah, this is part of who I am and I take it to myself, I accept it as part of myself—I will now keep it, deal with it, treasure it, for it is part of who I am. I will move on now for I no longer wonder if I can accept for I have completed that action." Now others can begin to do the same. Just show them how—show them this sign.

You may want to ask me, "Do you like being so hard of hearing?" The answer would be, no. But being hard of hearing has afforded me a fresh outlook, a sensitivity that might not have developed otherwise.

Others certainly do not choose to lose their vision, or the ability to walk or speak, or the sense of touch. Hopefully we can dwell on what we can do, what ability we do have. Thus, accepting life as it is, not as we might want it to be.

Think about choosing the road less traveled, think about the challenges and the bridges of understanding that can be built—even if the world thinks you are a bit foolish. We are in this world for such a brief time. Our lives are a gift. If the focus is on the precious moments, the everyday miracles . . . it all starts to make sense—moment by moment.

Life Is a Trip

I have met many people who were either losing their hearing, like I was, or had lost it all, and Frost's poem spoke to me. My view of the poem has changed as my perspective has changed over time. Growing older brings new insights as I encounter all sorts of life experiences. My philosophy and views have changed as I have aged, and it feels good—it's comforting to know I am not stagnating. Frost could have chosen either road because they weren't that different, but he had to choose one when he came to the fork in the road. He could not travel both at the same time.

True—we choose a path and the walk may not be easy. No matter which path we travel, we still need to learn how to cope with what life throws at us. Losing my hearing was tossed my way, and later multiple sclerosis (MS) was put on my plate. I choose to keep a positive attitude, no matter the circumstance, which is right for me—may be my destiny. You may think that I look at life through rose-colored glasses, but I believe my choice to see the positive side of life is better than my remaining a grumpy pessimist. Sure I have my blue days and I sink back into my old habits. I just don't stay there long.

Now, with a cochlear implant, I have been told I hear *and* understand more than 95 percent of sounds in relatively quiet settings. I hear new sounds continually, delighting in each one.

Remembering that hindsight is largely 20/20, if I had to choose my path again today for the first time, I would go the same way. Even though I had a fear of the unknown and felt that the flatlands were like mountains, I grew stronger when everything was not handed to me. Now, I realize no matter what path I had chosen—the open, clear path or the one with obvious obstacles—I would have matured and learned. Most of the time I have learned the hard way by jumping into situations without looking where I would land and wishing I'd asked more questions before my feet were engulfed in mud. I don't give up easily and I trust implicitly that God is leading me. Maybe He chuckles when I jump so fast, but He still teaches me.

When my daughter Mary was seven or eight, her secondary teeth were growing in crooked. She was upset because other children made fun of her and called her names. I remember her sitting at the top of the basement stairs while I exercised, her face hung low in her hands. I didn't know what to say. For the first time, I experienced the pain of watching my child in agony, and I knew that my words could make or break this part of her personality.

My response was not earth shaking, but she and I still remember it all these years later. "Mary," I said, "life is a tough road. If you walked along on even ground with no inclines and never felt bumps, you would never build strength. You wouldn't be able to climb. One thing I can tell you, Mary, is to remember what you feel like when people are cruel and don't ever do that yourself."

Mary now has three children and her two oldest currently have the same problem with their teeth. We recently laughed about this memory while on the phone. I remarked that it was good she knew how her children felt because she had walked the same rough road in her own childhood.

I Can't Hear You
When I Yawn

In 1998, I took a chance on sending an essay called "I Can't Hear You When I Yawn" to *Suburban News Publications* (*SNP*), a local newspaper in Columbus, Ohio. I'm still not sure to this day what moved me to do this. At the time, however, I knew my life was closing in and becoming smaller as I continued losing my hearing. The fog of my hearing loss and its related anguish in my daily life seemed to lift slightly when I wrote the words in coherent thoughts. Sending my writing to *SNP* was one risk of many I took as I became tired of battling my hearing loss and searched quietly, no pun intended, for a way to deal with it. Back then, I used a teletypewriter, or TTY, as it's more commonly called, to converse with people on the telephone. The TTY has a cradle for the telephone receiver, a small keyboard for typing messages, and a screen to read the messages. Cliff Wiltshire, the commentary editor at *SNP* at the time, called me through the Ohio relay service a few days later wanting to confirm that I had, in fact, written the piece he'd received in the mail.

I remember that my mouth hung open as his name came across the small TTY screen, and I realized that this was the first TTY call I had ever received from a nonfamily member. I liked this man instantly. When he said my piece was very good and barely needed editing, I think I blushed. For the first time, I was filled with anticipation of the unknown instead of fear, my usual silent partner.

My excitement bubbled over when I saw my newly published newspaper column, which appears below, along with my name listed as guest columnist; I knew something good was finally happening to me.

SHHH—*Hearing Loss Doesn't Need to Imprison People*

January 28, 1998

I can't hear you when I yawn. Or, for that matter, when I lean over . . . maybe because I cannot read your lips—I'm not quite sure. To hear you, or understand you, I need to face you and it helps to know what topic we are discussing. The weather? A movie? Work?

While other students were learning French or Latin, I was a self-taught student in lipreading and body language. These are all coping mechanisms I have learned to survive as a hard of hearing individual in a hearing, and noisy, world. Before I got my first hearing aid, I had no idea how loud train whistles, traffic, overhead announcements in stores, music (in church or concerts) were. Noise hurts my ears but I have an advantage over many. I can turn my hearing aids off and retreat into my silent world.

Take note, I did not say sad or lonely, but silent. I have grown to enjoy the silence and have lost all fear of potential deafness. How did I do that? I have been learning American Sign Language. I purchased a TTY. I utilize the Ohio Relay Service (ORS) and FM listening systems. I have an alarm clock that wakes me with a light and a smoke alarm people tell me could wake the dead. And I own a darling hearing dog, Snert. [More about him later.]

I have educated myself, my family, friends and coworkers. To do this, I listened to many people—hard of hearing, Deaf, and hearing—about their lives and how they have developed coping mechanisms for their obstacles, because everyone has them. I have read journals on hearing loss, watched programs on educational television, and learned to draw on my personal resources to redefine who I am without much hearing.

I have been a musician for years: singing, playing the guitar, piano and dulcimer, writing music and poetry and even recording some of my music. As my hearing gradually lessened, I withdrew from what was familiar including people, places and interests. This grew lonely and I decided I must accept my loss because it was not returning. This was difficult and to say differently would be a lie. Tumultuous is the best word to describe that time in my life.

The best way of coping for me has been my sense of humor. Often I say, with a big smile, "Do you want to know what I think you said?" It is like the game charades; "sounds like" but no cigar for her. I can honestly say, when I am asked if I have heard some gossip tidbits, "Nope," and thus that grapevine is eliminated where I stand.

I am blessed with an understanding family and place of employment; people meet me in the middle as much as possible. Therefore, I am not constantly walking 100% to meet them and everyone is happier and more comfortable.

Mourning a Passing Friend

I had sung in choirs ever since I was old enough to participate. Singing was fun and easy for me. Music was a talent in my family. I not only inherited this skill but have also passed it on to my daughter and grandchildren.

When I was a teenager, song lyrics eluded me. Remember the song "Blue Velvet" written by Bernie Wayne and Lee Morris? Bobby Vinton had a hit with it back in the summer of 1963. I loved that song. For years, however, I sang it as "Blue Melvin" because that is what the song title sounded like to me. Imagine my surprise years later when I heard the song again, but with my hearing aids on, and learned that it was about a blue velvet dress! I had thought all that time that poor Melvin was blue! My brother Jim and I laugh easily about this now.

When I was a Girl Scout, I loved camping and singing camp songs. Sometimes, though, I thought the songs had very strange titles. One night the troop leader asked me to lead a sing-along of "Whatcha Cut." I asked another camper what "Whatcha Cut" meant, and she told me that the song title was really "Watch of God." I had been singing, "Living in tents and cabins, under the 'whatcha cut, . . .'" thinking it was a hut or something like that before I fully understood the song lyrics.

When I attended college at Bowling Green State University during the 1960s, the music wafting out of the dorm room windows ranged from the Beach Boys to Judy Collins to Janis Joplin. My upbringing in a small town had not prepared me for all the musical diversity I heard in college, but I thrived on it. Folk music was also all the rage in the late 'sixties and early seventies. I even cranked out some folk music now and then on my guitar. I call it my "Peter, Paul, and Mary" era.

My ability to simultaneously play the guitar and sing faded as my hearing subsided in my thirties and forties. After I recorded some music I had written for safekeeping, I gave up the singing I had done most my life because I could no longer hear myself singing in a group and was certain I was no longer singing on pitch.

To Be Honest, I Really Do Miss Music

April 11, 2001

I admit it, I lied. I didn't realize this at the time, so maybe that gets me off the hook.

Many of my earlier columns were about losing my hearing, giving up things in my life and accepting these changes. One of those changes was the ability to enjoy music. I have lost too much of my hearing to hear subtle differences in tones so that singing or enjoying close four-part harmony is no longer possible. I choose to listen to tapes or CDs of music that I knew years ago.

I listen to the local oldies station WMNI-920 AM, where announcers know how to communicate without rambling and have wonderfully deep voices. I can even catch some news on that station. One evening I was listening to music while driving to a meeting. The songs were old folk songs and when they played "100 Miles," I began singing along. Memories of sitting around campfires, strumming my guitar and picking out these tried and true folk songs flooded my brain. Our voices would echo in the night.

I realized at that moment that I had lied to myself and to my readers when I said I didn't really miss music. I did, I admit it. Performing is not what I miss, but enjoying music in a concert or on the stereo is what I want to be able to do again.

This winter, my husband and I went to a Columbus Jazz Orchestra concert. The Palace has FM listening systems for hearing-impaired folks like me and I eagerly borrowed one, took my seat and waited. I was so excited to hear the Platters and listen to the Jazz Orchestra for the first time.

Bob kept glancing at me when everyone was laughing at the performers' jokes and he realized I was not laughing. When he told me, I returned the FM system and thanked them profusely for having so many devices available, but explained my hearing loss was too profound for the device to help. They were very sweet and understanding. I returned to more laughter and confusion. Wondering what they were saying, I tried to remember all my writings about acceptance, moving on, living with hearing loss and all my pep talks. I realized my own advice was failing me. When I write, you cannot see my face and my face tells whether I am lying, confused, lost or happy.

Bob knew I was lost and nothing he could do would help. Then the Platters stepped on stage and started singing "Only You." The audience joined them in song and so did I, thinking that with at least 1,000 people singing, no one was listening to me. I loved it.

But driving in my car, listening to "100 Miles" sung in the tone of the soft, reflective mood of folk songs I had loved, tears began to flow. I realized I had come to another crossroads and knew I had lied to myself. The words easily escaped my lips as I voiced, "I have been lying, I better write about this." It was a new kind of inspiration: deep-down honesty.

I wish there was something that could "make me hear" properly again, something that could allow me to listen without strain and laugh when others laugh. I wish I did not need to wear hearing aids or ask people to face me or repeat their words. Hey, we live in the real world, right? That just "ain't gonna happen" in my lifetime. The most

recent technology, called cochlear implants, cannot promise the fulfillment of this wish.

So my focus remains on what I can do, what I can enjoy. That is almost everything else in this life—fresh air, children, family, people,
diversity, home-baked bread, good writing and, above all, honesty.
Yes, I admit it. I miss music big time, but it is true that music plays in
my head and I can enjoy instrumental music, watching people dance
and children moving to music.

I asked Bob if I could still sing and carry a tune. His response was
thought out and kind—and honest: "I used to love to hear you sing
because it was mellow and smooth. Now I love to read your writing for the same reasons." I can't really sing well anymore so I opt to
sing to my grandchildren, in the car when no one is listening, or in a
large, loud crowd.

My Friend, Music

Like an old friend that had to depart
My music remains, in my heart.
For many years I performed, with my guitar in hand
Once on the radio and once with a band,
I sang in churches, at rest homes and camps
Loving to make all those people smile
Sharing the music that God generously inspired.
God also was listening and guiding my steps
Knowing the time to cease did exist.
Now my music is silent but it dwells in my heart.
God all around me and in my soul
The music is His and it made me feel whole.
Now the silence is blessed, difficult to understand
Sympathy easily can get out of hand.
If sadness comes near you and tugs at your heart
Remember these words so tears may not start.
My joy, love and pain are expressed in my songs
And God, in His mercy, can never be wrong.

November 25, 1997

Learning to Love Silence

Silence is very personal for me. I may have been selfish during the period when I learned to love silence, but it seemed a matter of survival at the time. I was learning not to fear the total absence of sound. I learned to become more visual when I took out my hearing aids. I found it was the best way to learn and practice American Sign Language (ASL). I had become accustomed to straining to catch small bits and pieces of spoken conversation whenever I wore my hearing aids. My ongoing habit of doing this while trying to learn ASL hampered my ability to pick up the language. Learning ASL became much simpler for me when I turned off the hearing aids.

I vividly remember the first time I went shopping without my hearing aids in the late 1990s. I was on my lunch break, walking toward Kohl's Department Store, when I decided to take out my hearing aids and put them in my jacket pocket. I knew that I would have an interesting experience no matter what happened. I was shopping for a dark red blouse. Most women know that looking for a specific item makes finding it next to impossible. It is only when we have no money that we find what we want. This day, though, I felt calm as I looked around the store. There was no PA system for me to misunderstand, no bothersome background music, and no clanking of hangers as other shoppers sifted through the racks of clothes. I smiled to myself as I sorted through the blouses and found two to try on. So far, so good.

As I headed for the dressing room, a clerk asked if I had found what I was looking for, or something like that—I was only reading her lips at this point. I replied with my stock answer that I was fine, thank you. I tried on the blouses and then headed for the check-out register. This is a moment when banter is common. I looked directly at the clerk and had my Kohl's card out before she asked how I was going to pay for my purchases. After I signed my receipt, she smiled and wished me well, and off I went. I felt like an adventurer and realized that I'd survived being in the hearing world while immersed in total silence, and I had even enjoyed it!

When in my personal realm of quiet, I could not communicate well with hearing people unless I chose to do so. I wasn't shutting myself out so much as I was learning to live in the deaf world. I use a small "d" since I was born hearing; I became deaf. People who are born deaf and/or grow up with ASL as their first language often describe themselves as Deaf. They have a rich culture that revolves around their language. Some people born deaf do not learn ASL; instead they speak and rely on lipreading. These people call themselves deaf. And then there are the folks like me who are hard of hearing and lose more hearing as we get older. We are deaf, not really Deaf. There is a real difference. I had to learn that I could survive in silence if I wanted the Deaf community to accept me. I desperately yearned for that acceptance because I never believed I would hear again. (I couldn't know that a cochlear implant would change my life in the future.) I was sure I would remain deaf, and I needed to find a way to accept living as such. In time, deafness didn't seem fearful to me and became almost comforting.

My Hearing Loss Affects Others around Me

What I did forget during this personal trial period is that my family and friends also struggled with my increasing deafness. I interpreted my deafness as a mere inconvenience for them, but I was wrong. It hurt them when I no longer sang in the choir or played my guitar. It was painful for them to see the look that came over my face as I pretended to know what was going on while trying to socialize in a group of hearing people. My daughter called it my "blank look." I was resigned to the fact that the hearing people could not understand the silence and perhaps did not want to. Again, I was wrong—at least, about some people.

One experience changed my outlook and prompted the following column.

Hearing Loss Can Affect the Lives of Those Around Us

January 20, 1999

We were standing in church. The organist was playing. Others were singing. My husband looked at me and motioned (in our private sign language), "Why aren't you singing?" I let him know I did not know the song. He stopped singing and looked forlorn. We proceeded to do what you are not supposed to do in church—we wrote notes back and forth. I am a lousy whisperer and cannot hear whispers.

For years, my husband had enjoyed my singing, especially with a good old gospel song. Over the years, my hearing ability has declined to the profoundly deaf level. Distinguishing different tones is very difficult. If I do not know a song well, I don't sing in public. And I don't sing unless many people are singing louder than me. I can't hear myself very well. I think this incident was my first vivid realization that my loss affects others. My hearing loss affects anyone with whom I communicate. Not just me.

My husband feels sad when I choose not to sing, knowing I love to sing. My daughter became quiet when I strummed my old guitar that I had given her. She said she missed my playing. Both of my daughters are teaching their children sign language. My son and one daughter use TTYs and on-line communication modes to stay in touch with me. Michael is in the Navy and is stationed in Hawaii. He makes a point of repeating to me whatever he had already told his Dad so I won't feel left out.

Other people affected by my hearing loss include clerks who patiently write down messages for me or turn the register display my way so that I can read the total amount due of my purchase. The airline flight attendants compensate by personally showing me the location of the emergency exits. And my co-workers have learned that they cannot easily pick up their phone and dial my extension to ask me a quick question. They must either dial me through the relay, send me an e-mail, or talk with me in person. A friend of mine who is recovering from surgery must wear a mask in public to protect herself. When she sees me, however, she removes the mask so I can read her lips. There are many who want to understand what my silence is like. These caring people hesitantly ask me question after question to figure out what I can actually hear.

My audiologist was affected when it was she who had to tell me that the problem was in my ears, and not with my hearing aids, when my hearing loss had taken another huge drop. She cried with me.

I wrote those incidences down in five minutes. If I took a long time to think, I could write all night. No one who knows me wants me to have this hearing loss. It affects them deeply. To deny this is unfair and unloving. In the past, I often accused people of sounding angry with me when they had to repeat something. Maybe they were angry. But not with me. Throughout the changes, we all had to learn to cope. It was painful. Sometimes the hearing loss is humorous—but always progressive.

Recently, I was listening to a choir. The music was ethereal. But my first impulse was to leave. I felt a pain that I could not bear or understand. But I remained and listened. I could have turned my hearing aids off but did not do so. Later, I told my daughter, Mary, that the emotion confused me. She said it sounded like a bittersweet experience. I got to thinking about that word—bittersweet. The plant is beautiful with bright orange berries, but tastes bitter. How like life is that word—bittersweet. Beauty mixed with pain, but coming through anyway, shining brightly like the plant. In the winter, the bittersweet is easy to spot amid the brown of the landscape. Lives can be that way, too.

Don't kid yourself. If you have a loss of a physical ability, it affects those around you. I want people to look at me, Liz, first, and then at my hearing loss, second. Most do. So, you may ask me why I keep writing about it, sharing, and educating you about what life is like with a hearing loss. Why not keep quiet, go sit in my office or den, and just get on with life? This is my way of getting on with my life. I want to help others who are struggling with this same inner grief that I have come through, and still experience at times. Sitting in my office and forgetting that my life, and the lives of those around me, has changed because I lost my ability to hear, serves no purpose. There must be a purpose for my having this loss.

So, yes, please do see Liz, or any person with a hearing loss, as a person first. But remember we hard of hearing folks have special needs in order to communicate effectively. We can do most things; we just can't hear very well. I urge all who are hard of hearing to remember that your loss affects others. Think about teaching others, gently, about what could improve everyone's quality of life. It is easy to become myopic about anything that affects us personally. It is happening to us, not "them." But it is also happening to "them."

Think about it. Don't kid yourself like I did. Work with hearing people to seek solutions. Communication will be more enjoyable. You will be easy to spot amid the busy landscape of life.

In time, I became more aware of others' reactions to my silence. I began to communicate my feelings and needs in different settings. Bob and I would work out cues or signs before we went to a crowded or noisy place. If I was talking too loud, which happened frequently, I asked Bob not to put his index finger to his mouth and make the "shhh" signal because this made me feel like a child whose parent was scolding her. Instead, we tried other cues like the sign for "soft(er)" or the sign for "quiet." Eventually, I developed an awareness of how loud I was by how my voice felt in my throat. I could also tell that I was too loud by looking at the facial expressions of my husband and other people I knew well.

Environmental Noise and Hearing Loss

I learned to tell people up front that I had a hearing loss or to say I was deaf without my hearing aids, particularly when I traveled alone. People were kind and offered more assistance most of the time when I did this.One such example was the time I needed a rental car at an airport. The service area was right next to the baggage claim. The loud conveyor belt noises and the luggage banging in the background made it almost impossible for me to hear the car rental agent. I coped with this situation by saying that I needed to see pictures of available cars so I could make a selection. The representative pulled out a flip chart from which I could select. When we finished the transaction, the agent told me that she also had trouble hearing in that work location, and was pleased to make this accommodation for me. My tactics actually saved time and de-stressed the situation for both of us. People have asked over the years if I became deaf from listening to loud rock music or if my deafness was the result of an illness. I sought answers to those questions over the years, only to come up empty-handed. Nerve deafness, the most common type, is the reason for my hearing loss. In my case, there is no explanation for why it happened. All I know is that some 15,000 hair cells in each of my cochlea—my inner ear—died over the years. Boom boxes and personal CD players did not appear until after I had grown up.

When I first used my hearing aids, I discovered that they amplify all sounds, regardless of whether those sounds are clear or muffled. I became sensitive to noisy environments and did not like hearing sounds I could not readily identify. I worried about losing the rest of my hearing, so I researched how I could preserve what hearing I still had. That research led to the following column.

Environment, Choices Can Lead to Hearing Loss
August 4, 1999

While driving home, I started talking out loud to myself—or was it to another driver? In any case, I did not have my hearing aids in. After I spoke, it occurred to me that I did not hear a thing. I kept talking louder and louder, understanding that I could only feel my voice, and not hear it. I must have been screaming before I could actually hear myself. "Wow," I thought, "I really am deaf."

It is not that I don't know that I am deaf without my hearing aids, I think I just forget. With the mechanical devices in my ears all day, I hear most noises and voices. True, I don't understand everything and must read lips to understand most words. But I do use my residual hearing. One thing I love to do is stand in a gentle breeze and feel the air. I can't remember when it happened, but I no longer can hear the sound of the wind.

I remember that I heard the wind for the first time in years when I got my first hearing aids at age 39. A normal windstorm was a terrifying experience for me because the noise was so loud that I thought a tornado was coming. My family assured me it was a normal summer storm. Now I only hear the wind through my hearing aids. If you have ever heard the wind whistle through a microphone at an outdoor event, you know what it sounds like to me. Now, I opt for the feel and fresh scent of the wind alone without the accompanying sounds.

Many sounds are no longer a part of my life. I still cannot avoid a lot of noise even though I have a significant hearing loss. It truly is a deafening world and getting more so every day.

There is an easy way to determine if the volume level is potentially hazardous to your hearing. If you are in a situation where you have to stand within three feet and yell to be heard, it is too loud. This kind of noise can damage your ears permanently. Imagine this scenario—it is a hot, summer day and you are mowing the lawn. A family member comes up to you, excitedly telling you something. The mower is still running—at about 90 decibels. You shout, "What?," in response to them. They repeat but you have not yet acquired good lipreading skills. You quickly turn the mower off in frustration, only to hear them shout, "I said, the dog just had six puppies!"

Protect your ears. If you don't, someday when you turn the mower off, you may not be able to hear what they say.

Sound is measured in decibels and each person has a different tolerance level to noise. The Occupational Safety and Health Administration (OSHA) set regulations for maximum exposure to noise on the job, in a typical 8-hour day, as 90 decibels in 1971 and revised in 1999 to 85 decibels.[1] Exposure to 85 decibels and above for long periods of time increases the risk of irreversible hearing loss. Here are some examples of different decibel levels:

Whisper, quiet library—30 decibels,
Quiet room—40 decibels,

---

1. OSHA Standard 1910.95.

Moderate rainfall—50 decibels,
Normal conversation, dishwasher—60 decibels,
Busy traffic, vacuum cleaner—70 decibels,
Alarm clock, busy street—80 decibels,
Lawnmower, shop tools, truck traffic, subway—90 decibels,
Snowmobile, chain saw, pneumatic drill—100 decibels,
Timpani and bass drum rolls—106 decibels,
Rock music, model airplane—110 decibels,
Jet plane take-off, amplified rock music at 4–6 feet, car stereo—120 decibels,
Firearms, air raid siren, jet engine—140 decibels,
Rock music peak—150 decibels.[2]

Young people are a new risk generation for noise-induced hearing loss. The popularity of listening to music at extremely loud levels for hours at a time increases the risk of permanent hearing loss. When one's ears ring or have a muffled sensation after a loud concert and one's hearing does not return to normal in 12–18 hours, the loss could be permanent.

Noise affects the entire body. Sudden, loud noise that interrupts a quiet situation can startle your whole body. It can cause your heart to race, your blood pressure to rise, your muscles to tense up, and your thoughts to be interrupted. You can constantly experience an overriding sense of anxiety if you're around a lot of noise often. You can become physically and emotionally drained as a result of this. Noise can cause stress, tension, difficulty sleeping, and irritability.

I do not wish hearing loss on anyone. There are more than 28 million people now who have some degree of hearing loss.[3] We comprise the largest disability group in this country. We should all consider ways we can decrease the amount of destructive noise in our environment. Most would agree that the future should hold good hearing for the majority of people rather than the reverse.

Often the marvelous sounds of nature, such as moving water, birds singing or trees rustling in the wind, or the peaceful quiet of the out-

2. From the American Speech, Hearing, and Language Association. www.asha.org.
3. Gallaudet Research Institute, accessed at http://gri.gallaudet.edu/Demographics/deaf-US.php.

doors, are obliterated by harsh, unnecessary noise. One does not nec-
essarily have to be hard of hearing to miss enjoying pleasant sounds
these days.

There is one simple, inexpensive solution when excessive noise
cannot be avoided—wear ear plugs. You can also lower the noise level
by turning down the radio, for example. You can also limit the amount
of time you expose your ears to loud noises. Protect your hearing.
Each of us can find ways to cut back on unnecessary noise daily. I encourage you to seek your own solutions and share them with others.

If you suspect you have trouble hearing, consider having it checked
by a licensed audiologist, especially if you like the sound of the wind.

You Are One
of Millions

The more I wrote columns related to hearing loss, the more letters I received. People wanted information, answers, and, most of all, people wanted out of their lonely, muffled world. Receiving these letters humbled me and gave a voice to readers. This also showed me I was doing what I was meant to do—write about what I know to reach out to others. I was learning about many lives different from mine other than our shared hearing loss. *SNP*'s copydesk secretary, Dorothy Stoyer, told me I received more letters than many other people. I'd see her short, curly-haired figure walking slowly toward my desk, smiling. Since she was metaphorically tied to her desk, having to answer phones and faxes, I knew the news was good as long as she smiled. She loved handing letters to me and saying, "Here's another one, Liz." Dorothy worked daily to help me succeed as a reporter by listening to my phone messages, taking detailed messages for me, and cueing me into the internal nuances of the newsroom. Her glee over the positive letters was a boost to my self-confidence.

Even though I am naturally gregarious, I had not yet found my niche as a whole person; I knew I had to break loose of my closed world, despite the onset of my deafness. My bluffing was not working well anymore, and with the support of friends like Dorothy, I became more true to myself. It would be impossible to count the times I floundered, answered questions incorrectly, and led conversations so I would know the topic. I felt as through I was constantly blushing from embarrassment throughout most of my adult life as a result of these mistakes. Through this personal pain, I learned how to advocate for myself and got better at explaining my hearing loss to others. The words flowing from my lips gradually became more natural; I began to understand myself more clearly as a deaf person.

Comments from hearing people who "just don't get it" can be painful. "Turn your hearing aids up," or one of my least favorite, "Oh, never mind." My knowledge of hearing loss continued to grow as my hearing spiraled down. I learned how lonely hearing loss can be even though my husband and grown children were patient.

I began learning sign language in my forties. My teachers were all born Deaf and several were raised in hearing families who did not learn sign language and primarily used speaking as the main mode of communication. The children born Deaf were taught to speak, which is considered oralism in Deaf Culture, and were discouraged from using signs. This was shown in the movie *Mr. Holland's Opus*. One of my teachers, Lori, told our class that even though she was born deaf to hearing parents, she was not allowed to use gestures to communicate. She was forced to function as an oral, deaf person until she was 16. I could see the pain on her face and later realized that she must have come to terms with this difficult part of her childhood as an adult because she did not elaborate further on this. I never discussed this with Lori, but I do know she was active in the first demonstration at Gallaudet University for the "Deaf President Now" rallies and she was proud of it. Maybe she moved on as an adult brushing the dust off her sandals as she walked away from her hearing family who forced oralism as her form of communication. If she reads my book, I hope I hear from her and learn the answer.

Lori was not alone in this pain. It was difficult for me to imagine not ever hearing your voice nor that of anyone else's, and having to learn to speak in a language you had never heard.

The column, "Hearing-Impaired people have lots of company," published in 1998, brought a letter that made me cry.

> March 15, 1998
> Dear Liz,
>
> I read your article with great interest yesterday afternoon in the German Village Gazette. I clipped your article out and put it in my coat pocket to respond to at a later time.
>
> That evening as I was riding with friends to a local restaurant, I asked one to repeat himself as I, too, am hard of hearing. All he responded with was, "Don't you have your hearing aids turned on?" When he said that, I had never felt so small. It was a slap in the face for me being who and what I am as a hard of hearing person.
>
> At the restaurant, while everyone was chatting away—it was hard to read their lips as the lights were poorly dimmed, I reached into my coat pocket in search of something else when I pulled out your article. I sat there reading and re-reading your words, "You're not alone."
>
> I've met quite a few other hard of hearing people and wanted us to be able to do things together, but most would rather not. Maybe they didn't want to be associated with one another. Then again, I do not know.
>
> I would <u>love</u> to be a member of SHHH. My concern is that the meeting might conflict with my work schedule . . . but I would also like to be able to participate in any social functions that the group has to offer.
>
> Thank you for your article and time.

This young man came to the next local SHHH meeting. He was delightful, verbal, and intelligent. He spoke openly about his work and concerns in front of the group. After he spoke, I strongly felt he was going to excel in his life.

I never saw him again, and hope he is doing well. If he reads this book, I hope he writes to me. He showed unusual strength and apparently got the boost he needed to persist in his life.

You're Not Alone . . . Hearing-Impaired People Have Lots of Company

March 11, 1998

"I felt alone, like I was the only one."

Hearing loss has created the largest disability group in the U.S. I would venture to say that those who have accepted their hearing loss and learned to cope with it would not consider it so much a disability as a shifting of gears. It's a case of refocusing ways to communicate effectively.

Don't get me wrong, most of us would not choose to be hard of hearing whether we have lost it gradually, over the years, or suddenly due to illness or trauma. But if we have done all we can to improve and protect what hearing we own, then we must learn to focus on what we can do versus what we can't do.

Imagine this—it is a warm, spring day. You are strolling along and a bright, red cardinal flies above and perches on a branch above your head. You stop, smile, and see the bird warbling a song, but, all of a sudden, you realize you can't hear it. You move closer, still no sound. The beauty does not cease because you cannot hear the song, it has just changed. Now your eyes are counting the beauty not your ears. How I love a spring day with its soft breezes, sweet fragrances of early flowers and trees blooming, and children racing down the street on their bikes. I see the kites flying high in the schoolyard behind our house and can hear laughter in my imagination. If you really look at the curves of the trees and touch the ragged bark, see the vivid and subtle colors of the sky and flowers, the branches swaying in the breeze, and feel the whoosh as a child rides her bike past you, beauty is surrounding you. Scents, sights, and touch bring the sounds alive in a new way.

Your grandchild hugs you and whispers in your ear. You don't know what she whispered but the softness of the hug lingers on your neck, and you whisper back tender words of love. Your love for that child has not diminished because you could not hear her words. This is what I call a shifting of gears or focus.

How could a person among 28 million feel alone? Easy. I did. Most do. You cannot see hearing loss. You can hide it, you can bluff your way through life, you can deny it but, most importantly, you can isolate yourself—drop out of life, find yourself alone, lost, and confused. You can think that there are no answers or solutions. But you would be wrong. I was wrong. Personally, I got fed up with loneliness and isolation. I wanted to communicate with my friends and family but did not know how to start that journey of discovery. I didn't know where to buy the ticket or how much it would cost. I was afraid. Many are. I understand and so do many others.

If you have read this far, you may be saying, "Who are these people who understand? How could anyone understand how I feel? How could anyone know how it feels to lose friends who don't want to try to communicate; how it feels to not have the money to buy hearing aids or an amplified phone? How could anyone know how it feels to sit alone night after night, frightened and frustrated, trying to think of a solution all by myself or how it feels to be left out of conversations or meetings because it seems that everyone is mumbling?"

The answer is simple, but the solutions are up to you. The people at Hearing Loss Association of America (formerly SHHH—Self Help for Hard of Hearing People) understand and care. They understand, and most have experienced what you are feeling at this moment. None of them want you to stay alone. They want to help you find the solutions to improve your life, to step forward, to refocus, and to dwell on what you can do.

Many of these same people are still searching for solutions and acceptance. You are not alone. But it is up to you to take the first step, leave your room, and "buy a ticket." Only then can you begin again to grow, learn, and accept. Self-help does not have to mean "poor me." You can choose to have it mean that there is hope, I can learn, and I can move on.

Not hearing conversations and some sounds can cause one to feel lonely in a crowd. My guess is most people in that crowd also feel alone. We each have our reasons. The idea of feeling excluded from the "norm" puts everyone in the same boat. How can we define normal? Is it even possible? Even a normal heartbeat can equal so many things—sounds, rhythm, and rate. A normal personality? Not possible to define.

You Can't Catch Deafness

Hearing loss is not contagious. It is not terminal, and it is not the end of life as we know it. It is a detour with barriers. Each time we clear a hurdle, we become stronger and more prepared for the next one.

Even so, we may wonder why there are so many people with hearing loss. I wrote the following poem for my friend Pat Vincent who is one step away from total deafness. Pat told me he had been thinking that God must love hard of hearing people, since he made so many of us. With millions, maybe he is right. Pat, always the encourager, asked me if I might write a poem based on this concept. I let him know he would be the first to read it if I was so inspired.

Why So Many?

Did God tap you on the shoulder?
Or call you by your name?
You say you cannot hear, that your ears are weak?
When He talks to you, do you think
That makes a difference to Him?
Surely He cares and we know He hears,
But where was He, you might ask,
When the sound of the wind became hushed and
Voices soon became a blur?
Do you think God might have heard?
Doubtless, He knows all our pain and
All of our questions, before we ask them of Him.
He loves every soul, we are His creation.
So why so many with their hearing diminished?
The world is so noisy, a regular din.

Do you think, in the silence, we are more focused on Him?
Without the distractions of this clamoring earth,
Do you think it is easier to have spiritual rebirth?
No one has the answers—if we keep our hearts directed above
Our lives will be overflowing with blessed, peaceful love.
With faith to carry and to sustain
While millions join hands to deal with the pain
And teach others how to, from anger, refrain.
Maybe in silence we now do exist
So that when we're in Heaven, in the choir, we will lift
Our voices with joy so the exalted sound
Will reach from the heavens right to the ground.

So let's rejoice in our stillness and listen for His voice;
There are more ways than hearing to make that choice.
Millions live in a quiet, hushed world;
God loves them all, to Him we are whole
It is a deafening silence but His arms encircle us all
With a love so warm it will soften our hearts.
Then we are ready to listen, not with hearing but from our soul;
Now, in our silence, our lives can be full.

November 30, 1997

Handling Hearing Loss During Hospital Stays or Medical Tests

Many people with hearing loss want to hide it from others, especially from hearing people. I met a salesman who took his hearing aids out before a sales call—and I asked how he heard the customer. "I manage," was the answer. One woman was going into the hospital for surgery. I reminded her to take extra hearing aid batteries with her. "Oh, I'm not taking my hearing aids. I don't want them to know." Then she added, after seeing my perplexed look, "My husband will hear for me." Knowing the woman quite well, I knew she could not be deterred but my gut reaction was, "Really?! At three in the morning?,"

No matter how I tried to convince her, she refused to change her mind. There are other instances where people went to great lengths to hide their hearing loss. Since I had tried to hide my hearing loss as I was growing up, the freedom I later felt to let others know was a great relief for me. When asked to write the following article for the Ohio Women with Disabilities Network, I incorporated some of the experiences I have just mentioned, and was glad to get the word out.

Work Together Toward Hospital Communication[1]

You are about to enter the hospital for a procedure and will be there anywhere from one to eight days. You are packing, deciding what to take. You remember that your hearing aid batteries usually last one week. Perhaps you should take extra ones. You hesitate. Maybe it would be better to leave the hearing aids at home and bluff your way through.

On the other hand, bluffing may not work for you, your family, or the hospital staff. Why add to the stress? You re-think your strategy. You put the batteries in the suitcase and add a few sharpened pencils and a big pad of paper. You have made a very "healthy" decision although it wasn't easy. You don't want to go to the hospital. You would much rather stay home. But this visit is unavoidable and necessary. Taking a deep breath, you finish packing.

During the hospital admission process, you tell others that you wear hearing aids. You ask them to:

- Please face you as they speak.
- Keep their hands and food away from their mouth so that you can read their lips.
- Write their comments with pen and paper you provide when you are unable to understand them.
- Provide a qualified sign language interpreter if you are deaf and communicate through sign language.

1. Elizabeth Thompson, "Work Together Toward Hospital Communication," *Window on Wellness*, Ohio Women with Disabilities Network, Spring 1999.

You feel good about yourself for making your communication needs known to the hospital staff. You have been a self-advocate.

That's what it is all about—communication. Legal Rights, The Guide for Deaf and Hard of Hearing People, states,

> It is not possible to have equal access to services without communication. Communication, is perhaps, the most important ingredient for health care. Without communication, the patient cannot explain the symptoms of his or her illness to the medical staff.
>
> Without communication, the patient cannot comprehend the routines of treatment or preventive medicine. If all medical patients were treated [poorly], the general population would be outraged. Yet deaf people face [lack of communication] these circumstances daily.[2]

Hospitals should, by this time, be aware that the Americans with Disabilities Act (ADA) states that public places, such as hospitals, must accommodate the needs of people who are hearing impaired. Specifically, Title III (Public Accommodations), states that:

> No individual shall be discriminated against on the basis of disability in the full and equal enjoyment of the goods, services, facilities, privileges, advantages, or accommodations of any place of public accommodation by any person who owns, leases (or leases to), or operates a place of public accommodation.[3]

This provision includes the requirement to make communication available. It may mean that if you are hearing impaired you will need the use of an amplified phone or a TTY or access to a sign language interpreter.[4] A pad and pencil may be the last resort. In a medical setting, particularly in a stressful setting such as a hospital, every effort should be made to make sure that the hard of hearing patient is able

2. National Association of the Deaf, *Legal Rights: The Guide for Deaf and Hard of Hearing People*, Washington, D.C.: Gallaudet University Press, Fifth edition, 2000, p. 101.

3. 42 U.S.C. 12182(a).

4. National Association of the Deaf, *Legal Rights: The Guide for Deaf and Hard of Hearing People*, Washington, D.C.: Gallaudet University Press, Fifth edition, 2000, pp. 30–34.

to communicate. Staff should be aware of and trained on how to communicate best with people with hearing disabilities.

When I had my first MRI, magnetic resonance imagery, I did not have hearing aids. I did not know what I would encounter. I was placed in a large tube and told to lay very still. For about forty minutes, I not only felt claustrophobic but also felt isolated, alone, and fearful. I was concerned about the outcome of the MRI. The technicians were continually speaking to me, but I couldn't hear them and had no idea what they were saying. It was a bad experience for me.

Seven years later I had another MRI. This time I had my hearing aids in, and I knew what to expect. I had also learned to tell people that I was hard of hearing. The test was again claustrophobic, but I felt more in control of the situation because the technicians were aware of my needs.

Recently while visiting someone in the hospital, I noted a crude sign on a patient's door that read, "Patient deaf." It was an impersonal sign written in crayon, almost as if it served as a warning rather than functioning as an aid in the patient's health care. I felt that the sign did not convey respect for the patient's dignity. I believe it is important for hospital staff to be aware when a patient is deaf. The patient's chart, bed, and intercom should be flagged appropriately so that staff knows when a patient is hard of hearing or deaf; needs hearing aids to hear; needs to be spoken to slowly; and/or uses an interpreter to communicate.

Again, it is incumbent upon hospital staff to be trained in working with deaf and hard of hearing people. If hospital staff wants patient cooperation during medical procedures, then patients must understand and be able to follow directions. If patients cannot understand what is happening, their medical care may be jeopardized.

Hospitals may want to purchase an inexpensive program called "Access 2000 and the 4-Point Program for Hospitals" from the Hearing Loss Association of America.[5] The program highlights four areas of concern—

- Technology
- Patient identification

5. The program is in the process of being converted from video format to DVD format and having its labeling changed from SHHH to HLAA to reflect the organization's name changes, but the new version should be available soon.

- Staff training
- Publicity

The program offers training to hospital staff in learning how to identify hard of hearing or deaf people and how to work with them. It shows them how other hospitals have effectively met the ADA requirements for patients who are deaf or hard of hearing. The program emphasizes that hospital staff and patients must work together. If patients enter the hospital and do not identify themselves as deaf or hard of hearing, then how can hospital staff pool resources to help make patient stays as medically helpful and stress free as possible.

A large minority of the 28 million-plus individuals with some degree of hearing loss in the United States refuse to be identified as "hearing-impaired." I prefer using the term "hard of hearing." Others prefer "deaf" or, capitalized "Deaf," or prefer to say, "I have a loss of hearing" or "I don't hear very well." I urge all who are hard of hearing (or whatever phrase you are comfortable with) to identify yourselves as such when you enter a hospital or when you have a medical test, especially in a situation in which you cannot see the technician, for example, during mammography, MRI, x-ray or CAT scan. Ask in advance if you need to remove your hearing aids during the tests and, if so, figure out an alternative way for communicating with technicians.

Some suggestions for hospital staff include the necessity of sensitizing personnel as to the special needs of people with hearing losses, such as the need to—

- Provide adequate, glare-free lighting.
- Control background noise for all hearing-aid wearers.
- Make needed visual modifications to auditory fire alarm systems.
- Change evaluation procedures which require speaking and hearing. Provide interpreters where required.
- Free a patient's hands and arms for signing and gesturing.

The upshot for deaf and hard of hearing people in medical situations is when you have individual needs, work with your healthcare providers to find solutions. You know what works best for you so don't be afraid to advocate for yourself. If you do these things and know your legal rights, you will be able to get proper treatment in medical facilities. It will end up as a win-win situation for you and for the health care personnel involved. I have learned that when I speak openly with medical technicians, nurses and doctors about my needs, they accommodate me beautifully. Even now, with a cochlear implant, my batteries can die, the device easily slips off my scalp and I am once again deaf.

The most significant experience I have had, proving that building internal habits of self-advocacy is important, was on December 1, 2005. We had moved to Ohio from Seattle and the basement was full of unpacked boxes. Because of my multiple sclerosis, stairs and I are not good friends. Even so, I chose to go downstairs and play seek-and-find with the myriad of boxes. Not only that, I decided to put things on the steps and take them up the stairs, one step at a time.

With my cane in my right hand, I used my left hand to "march" the boxes up the steps and shove them on the kitchen floor. But when I reached the second step from the top, my balance proved unworthy and I started falling backwards. Falling down all of nine steps, which I counted days later, I felt sure I would not survive and the last thing I remember was yelling, "Oh my God." Some unknown minutes later, I woke up with a broken right arm and a cell phone that would not work in the basement.

To make a long story short, somehow I pulled and pushed my body up to the very step I fell from and called 9-1-1. I told the operator where the EMS people could enter the house. With my back to the life-saving team, I quickly told them I had a cochlear implant and if the batteries died, I would be instantly deaf.

Barb Brown, a neighbor I had met once, came over to help and she called my husband's cell phone. She also cared for our dogs that entire day as I was in the hospital. I asked her to get the box of batteries from the kitchen drawer and I took them with me. How I was clear headed enough to think of that had to be that I had ingrained tactics inside to tell and explain quickly. It was second nature. Later in the Emergency Room, I repeated this talk with the technicians doing x-rays and the CAT Scan, even though by then I was in shock. I also wear a medical ID necklace telling of my implant in my right ear.

I broke my arm, dislocated my shoulder and was bruised for weeks—but I survived and my advocacy is stronger today after this experience. You never know. Make it an internal language and it will spill out when needed. I promise.

Handling Insensitive Questions and Changing One's Attitude

As a deaf or hard of hearing person, have other people ever asked such an insolent question that it totally amazes you as to the amount of ignorance and misunderstanding it conveys? Our first reaction might be to think that it is possible that we have misunderstood the question or misread its meaning. It is easy for us as deaf or hard of hearing people to blame ourselves, thinking, "They couldn't have said that." Or you might think to yourself, "What did I do to cause them to think in such a way that they would even ask such a question?"

I am careful how I word my own remarks because I have, in fact, been the recipient of many insensitive comments or questions over the years. If I tell someone, "Oh, you got your hair cut!" and say nothing more, I then recoil at the thought that my comment might be negatively misconstrued, and quickly go on to add, "And it looks good." I'm not referring to people who ask questions like, "When is the baby due?" and you're not pregnant. I'm talking about people who unwittingly say, "What do you mean you can't hear me? Are you deaf?" or, my least favorite, "Gee, I wish I could turn off the noise once in awhile. It must be nice."

No, it is not nice. It's difficult living in a hearing world, in which noise drowns out vocal clarity. It is annoying for us when background noise, such as a soft drink machine's humming or copier noise, means that we have to tell someone, "I can't hear you."

But in my senior year of high school, my English teacher, Ms. Boyd, asked us if you had to choose, would you rather lose your hearing or your vision? This question has never left my mind and inspired the following column.

Some Difficult Questions Should Never Be Asked

"If you had to choose, would you rather lose your hearing or your vision?" What a question! I was 17 years old and a high school senior, when our English teacher posed this question to our class. I wanted to ignore it, but she wanted an answer. I thought about it. I had just "starred" in our senior musical. I loved to sing and listen to music. Music is probably the reason I survived high school.

She looked at me and said, "Well, we all know Liz that you would choose to lose your vision. You would then still be able to hear music." Had she read my mind? No. Now I am about the same age she was then and I wonder if I would pose that question to anyone. I know people with perfect vision and low or no vision, people who hear everything, and those who have hearing losses that range from mildly hard of hearing to deaf. I know people who power walk and run marathons and others who struggle to place one foot in front of the other. Their own kind of daily marathon. There are people who cannot lean over due to back injury and gymnasts who jump and bend in midair.

Well, you could add your own struggle or triumph here couldn't you? Would you appreciate this question? Again, I think not. With maturity, I have learned what I wish I could tactfully have said to my teacher and probably not gotten into trouble for having said it. I would say that I'd choose not to lose either sense and that I felt that the question and accompanying comment were insensitive. How could any one loss be worse or better than another?

But her question has stayed with me some 30 years later. As my hearing gradually waned over the years, I often wondered why. See, I agreed with the teacher when she said I would not want to lose my hearing. But I did lose it. So now what do I do? The teacher didn't waste time discussing what we'd do if we lost one or the other sense I had to ask new questions. Find new ways to cope. Make new friends who understood my situation. It took time and energy. I often fell back, gave up, and had to regroup. Since my hearing declined slowly, I had years to hear most things and enjoy music. I still enjoy instrumental music, not vocal music because the words just don't come across anymore for me.

I love music programs on television that are closed-captioned. The best of two worlds. Often, I wish people were closed-captioned. The journey has not been easy and, in hindsight, I would have done many things differently. You, the reader, may be struggling with some sort of loss—vision, hearing, sense of touch, ability to move with some amount of grace, taste. I don't need to tell you how to cope with it unless I have lived it myself.

Even then, each of us has to find our own way, consistent with our lifestyle and needs. A bridge certainly exists, between people who have lost the use of one or more senses. We have all been asked unfeeling questions and felt compelled to answer. But maybe the questions hit closer to home. We are dealing with a friend or family member who shows insensitivity to our needs.

When this happens, we become the teacher. We ask the questions and let them know what we need, "Please face me; please don't talk to me from another room." [If they are stubborn and refuse to comply, they are the ones with a problem. Not you. Many choose to ignore the situation. You may be a vivid reminder for them that it "could be them" someday. I just smile and say, "But it isn't you, right now it's me." And I continue trying to build that bridge of understanding.]

People are generally kind-hearted. I need to let them know. I become the teacher.

My high school teacher had a purpose in her question. I will allow you to draw your own conclusions. Thirty years later, I have become the teacher. But with the questions, I am willing to find answers that help improve the quality of my life.

The Hearing Loss Association of America has been the best school I have ever attended. While the organization is not a building, it is an entity that offers education on coping with hearing loss. The other pupils are either hard of hearing or those who want to understand. You may be taking the first step toward coping by learning there are people who understand, people who care, and who will help guide you toward the answers required to improve your life. They have helped me to answer my big question. "Now what?"

Discovering My MS

I believe most people have a "condition" to live with that is hidden. My first indication that something else might be wrong with me in addition to my hearing was when I was fourteen years old. My right hand was paralyzed for about ten minutes. I still remember that it was summer and I was wearing cut-off jeans and a T-shirt. I was in the dark family room trying to get cool sitting on the high-backed, wooden couch that had been my grandmother's. I sat still and waited until the paralysis passed. The next time I experienced something odd was when I was eighteen and in college. Fatigue overwhelmed me and moving was an effort. I went to the infirmary, where they tested my blood. The nurse said that she thought I had mononucleosis even though the blood work didn't indicate it. The only instructions were to rest and not to kiss anyone. About six weeks later, the fatigue was gone and I was fine.

My right side went completely numb when I was about eight weeks into my pregnancy at age twenty-two. I felt as if a line had been drawn from the top of my head down to my foot. My entire right side had no feeling. I went to the doctor about this and his wisdom floored me. His only comment was, "Your bra is too tight." Honest. That is what he said. I asked what that had to do with my tongue being numb and he had no answers.

For years after this, I would fall for no apparent reason, would occasionally walk veering to the right, and I would feel unusually tired the rest of the day after a workout or a jog. Once, I fell asleep at my typewriter.

Our family had just moved to Kent, Washington in 1987, and I was finally able to be a stay-at-home mom for the first time ever. Our children were thirteen, fifteen, and seventeen at the time. We visited churches to find a church home. We were sitting in a church pew about two weeks after we arrived in Kent, and I turned to look at my husband. "Where had he gone?" I wondered. I had to do a full body turn in order to see him. I had overcome a horrific migraine the day before, and was under a lot of stress from all the recent changes.

I went to a nearby optometrist, Dr. Green, to get my eyes checked because I thought that my contacts were bad. It was the most thorough eye exam I had had in a long time. He gave me a field vision test, which seemed like the then-popular Star Wars game to me. I pressed a handle whenever I saw a flashing object.

Dr. Green brought me the results and said he had just gotten off the phone with a well-known neurologist in Seattle, a Dr. Craig Smith. "I made an appointment for you. He wants your husband to come as well." Dr. Green said, "I think you are having a series of strokes."

"But I am only thirty-six," I thought at the time, as my mind whirled in a tizzy of disbelief. He told us to keep the appointment and we did.

Dr. Smith gave me a neurological exam, put me on a regimen of beta blockers and aspirin to ward off further migraines, and told me to call if any new symptoms occurred. The fact that I might be having a series of strokes baffled both my husband and myself. I had several appointments with Dr. Smith during the next few months. At one of these appointments, the doctor asked me if I knew anything about MS.

"No," I replied.

Then I did a silly thing. I went to the library, looked up "MS," and found nothing. I did this research before the days of the Internet. I occasionally had slurred speech and trouble walking over the next several months. I also had periods when I could not read a series of numbers correctly and experienced numbness in various spots on the right side of my body.

Then the worst occurred. I counted more than seven different symptoms of MS at one time and panicked. I called Dr. Smith's office, thinking I was having a massive stroke. He set up an MRI for the next morning. His parting instructions were, "Tell them you are to bring your film with you and come up to my office. Bring Bob with you."

The MRI showed one large lesion in my left brain, along with some other smaller ones. The lesions showed on the MRI film as white spots while the rest of the film was black or outlines of a section of my brain. He showed me the lesions and explained that I had Multiple Sclerosis.

You might think this odd, but I was relieved.

I asked, "Can it kill me?"

"Not if you take care of yourself," he said.

"Teach me then what to do," I replied earnestly.

I was at the beginning of the road in learning about MS and about its effects on my body—a journey I never could have anticipated. My having had to cope with a gradual hearing loss was good training in my learning to cope with MS. My hearing had died slowly, and now my body functions were also fading.

Cultivating a More Positive Attitude

One day I was weeding my flower garden and I felt thankful for having become deaf and for having Multiple Sclerosis. I don't always feel thankful every day, but I learned that day that doing simple chores at times can help foster this gratitude. That experience inspired the following column

Weeding Can Be Good for What Ails You.

June 21, 2000

Heat and humidity can cause moisture build-up in hearing aids and can lead to longer-term damage. Getting myself overheated contributed to my experiencing uncontrollable fatigue due to the fact I have MS. But the sunshine was beckoning me to go outside and garden. So I took my hearing aids out, drank a big glass of ice water, put my dog on a long leash, and gathered my gardening tools. I donned my working gloves and sat in the grass, still moist from dew. The silence engulfed me like a thick sweater on a cold night. I started weeding and looked over at my dog lying in the shade of the tall, yet-to-be mown grass. He was sniffing the air with fervor.

I found myself smiling and continued to pull weeds from in between the flowers. It was getting too warm for me to stay outside pulling weeds. Suddenly, I felt a cool, refreshing breeze. I realized at that moment that I was glad I had become deaf and that the MS had urged me to sit while weeding. These two physical facts of my life had slowed me down enough to notice the breeze, take a moment and see the sky was a clear blue, and to take my time with this task. The weeds weren't going anywhere. I could always return and finish the job later.

A friend asked me to write a few paragraphs about how I keep such a positive attitude regarding my MS for her book. This request came while I was having a big self-pity party. I accepted her challenge and was surprised when I found myself writing that I believe you can hear peace. My deafness has allowed me the opportunity to learn how to listen in new ways. My MS has taught me how to pace myself by moving more deliberately.

I wrote that I can hear peace—it might be better explained if I say that I can feel peace. I can feel the silence, feel the breeze and the sun, feel the blessings that come my way, especially when life hadn't turned out the way I'd planned.

How can I be grateful for deafness or MS, or any other "limitation" for that matter? What can I do about it? Even if I get a cochlear implant, there is no guarantee that I will be able to hear. It doesn't rule out my getting one in the future. But, in the meantime, I have learned to love silence. Most people born deaf don't see their deafness as something that needs to "be fixed," but that it is a part of who they are. At this moment, I finally understand that. I always appreciated it before, but now I finally understand what it means.

MS is elusive and unpredictable. It is different for each person—no cause is known and no cure has been found—yet. But there are ways to learn how to "manage" the disease. That is what I am determined to do. I am learning what works for me, talking with others who have MS—they are not hard to find—and I am using the Internet to keep abreast of the latest information about MS. The best web site I have found so far is www.MSWorld.org. That site has message boards for talking with others with MS, monitored chats, information libraries, along with articles and poems written by people living with MS. With understanding, manageability becomes possible.

I have decided that I am, in fact, in charge of my attitude, just as Charles Swindoll wrote—

> The longer I live, the more I realize the impact of attitude on life. Attitude, to me, is more important than facts. It is more important than the past, than education, than money, than circumstances, than failures, than successes, than what other people think or say or do. It is more important than appearance, giftedness or skill. It will make or break a company, a church, a home. The remarkable thing is we have a choice every day regarding the attitude we will embrace for that day. We cannot change our past, we cannot change the fact that people will act in a certain way. We cannot change the inevitable. The only thing we can do is play on the one string we have, and that is our attitude. I am convinced that life is 10 percent what happens to me and 90 percent how I react to it. And so it is with you, we are in charge of our attitudes.

No matter what the topic is, my attitude will decide how I react. Bitterness or anger toward my "special" abilities does not enter my heart very often. When I find myself throwing a pity party just for me,

I realize it is very lonely. If I were to drag others into it, then I would be surrounded by lots of depressed people. I prefer to stay positive and surround myself with others who have learned to adapt to their individual circumstances.

I have a suggestion for the next time you feel like throwing a pity party for one. Go outside, feel the breeze, and pull a few weeds from your soul's garden. It did wonders for me and I hope it also helps you.

What's Your Shoe Size?

I have small feet and maybe that explains why few people have tried to walk in my shoes. But this chapter really isn't about shoe size. Instead it is about trying to see someone else's life through his or her eyes. An old Indian proverb I have heard goes something like, "Don't judge a man until you have walked a mile in his shoes." This is my take on that quote.

My Growing Up Years

Families are a group of people who care about and protect each other. We don't choose our family, we are either born or adopted into it. Sometimes it is the luck of the draw or a God-send to even have a family at all.

I was born on September 11, 1951 into a family with two older brothers, Jim and Jon, and, later, a younger sister, Cynthia. Growing up in a small town, Westerville, Ohio, during the fifties was, obviously, different from today. My home did not have locked doors or air conditioning. The only key I owned was a skate key that hung on a piece of grubby string that I wore around my neck. My summers included days of swimming, running, biking, skating and sleeping on clean, white sheets on warm nights while the oscillating fan hummed me to sleep. Life was easy and carefree.

I wanted to be like my brothers—to run faster and swim harder—so you can imagine me as a tomboy, growing up. Our family was not perfect, but I had one and we all did our best. The Church of Messiah United Methodist was a focal point for me both as a girl and as an adult. I wore a white robe that sported a big, red bow at the neck when I participated in the cherub choir as a girl. Later, I sang in "Helen's Angels," a sextet including Gretchen and Trina Steck, Maryann Gill, Janice Wells, Patty Beth Lord, and me. We laughed and sang to the delightful direction of Helen Swank. Singing and music was my creative outlet. It made me feel intimately connected with other people and, thus, complete.

I could no longer discern musical pitches by the time I was forty-three, at which point I had to stop singing in choirs. I literally could not hear myself or the person next to me to know if I was on pitch. I recorded all the songs I'd written and gave my guitar to my daughter Mary. I let that phase of my life end, but not without feeling pain over it.

I was at my nephew Chris's wedding reception in 1998 and the music was loud. People were dancing happily and having a great time. My brother Jon approached me with an odd look on his face and proceeded to shout a question to me that I later used for the following column.

Understanding Comes from Wearing Other's Shoes

September 1998

"Can you hear that, Liz?" my older brother asked me. We were at his son's wedding reception and the disc jockey was playing great music. The DJ had just made an announcement and, thinking that this is what my brother meant, I answered, "Yes, but I can't understand his words."

Jon clarified the question, "Can you hear the music?"

I gave him a big smile and said, "Oh yes . . . even without my hearing aids." We then laughed.

Later I realized that the real purpose of his question was not so much "Can you hear it?" but "How much of it can you hear?" I loved Jon all the more when I realized the intent behind his question. He was trying to walk in my shoes—trying to understand deafness since he had never experienced it. Hearing loss is invisible to the eye. My brother was going to great lengths to try and comprehend what I could hear because he could not see it.

Some people have said of me, "But she looks normal." Very funny. Define normal for me, will you? Being hard of hearing is normal for me. In fact, it is normal for millions of people. So we are normal; we just can't hear very well. What hard of hearing individuals would love to hear more of are sensitive questions like that of my brother Jon. We hard of hearing people welcome those kinds of questions that reflect a genuine effort to empathize with our situation. Some hearing people balk at using the Ohio Relay Serve, a marvelous, free service provided in all states so that hearing people can call someone who uses a TTY.

I asked my oldest brother, Jim, if he minded talking to me using the service not long after my experience at the wedding.

"No," he said, "Even if I did, what difference does it make as long as I can communicate with you?" I had to stifle the tears. I probably should have let them flow. What an honor to have brothers like mine!

I first had to accept my loss before I could gain independence in the hearing world. That was the most difficult part. Think, for example, of what it's like when you start an exercise program. I had to force myself to learn, to fall, then get up, and start the mental exercise of motivating myself to continue. Whew! It wore me out, but I felt energized afterwards. I "got into shape" but continue to "work out" to maintain my current fitness level. I am still learning.

Second, I learned about assistive listening devices. The best example is having my dog trained through Lion's Hearing Dogs to serve as my hearing dog. That was fun. Third, I had to practice using these devices regularly to improve my quality of life. Fourth, I had to teach people daily what I need for optimum communication. That process will never end, which is fine because teaching and learning are always good things.

I also used writing throughout all these phases as a way of helping me put my situation in perspective. I also hope that my writing helps others through their own healing process. All I ask is that you make an effort to understand—to walk in my shoes—even just for a short time. I think I speak for millions of hard of hearing people when I say I want to hear and understand you, but I often can't. I also ask for your patience as we work on communicating with one another. Humor often dispels the communication gap as we let others into our silent world with welcoming arms, a laugh, or a smile.

Then, the next time the music blasts and someone wonders if you can hear it, you can laugh and say, "Oh, yes!"

Approaching Deafness

Telling others that you have a hearing loss can be downright impossible for some people. It took me time to find the right words, especially when I talked with strangers about it. If I said I was hard of hearing, many people didn't grasp the extent of the loss and tended to shout at me, which only served to distort sounds even more for me. Then, I started saying I was deaf without my hearing aids—bingo! People seemed to understand that, but would then question my ability to speak well. I attributed my clear speech to all of the music training I'd had over the years. All of the training in clearly enunciating consonants helped keep my speech understandable as I was losing my hearing.

My speech was so clear, in fact, that when I arrived in college to study music that my voice teacher, Rex Eikum, said my diction was too good and he would have to "slop" my speech down a little. Amazing.

As I neared the point of total deafness, I and others noticed that I was not finishing words all the time and that my voice had become more guttural and huskier-sounding. I learned later that my vocal changes were survival techniques I had unconsciously employed so that I could still "hear," or feel, my voice. Songs ran through my mind almost constantly. Who knows—I may have been humming them and not realizing it at the time. I often wonder what other sounds I might have made back then that I could not hear but were discernible to others. You can use your imagination here because I don't like to think about it.

Stories of Growing up Deaf in a Hearing Family

It was 2005, Bob and I had moved to Monroe, Washington, from Phoenix. Lush green contrasted with the desert we left behind. We rented a Cape Cod–style home in the country with several acres surrounded by vast, wild blackberry bushes and pine trees so tall the tops seemed to touch the clouds. Our time here was quiet and friendly. I continued to write for *Hearing Health Magazine*.

A story I wrote about a Seattle girl and her father caught the eye of Karen Stueland, who lived and worked in Seattle. She sent me an e-mail from her work place, which was a speech and hearing center and we kept "talking." I think I can discern through e-mail when a person is interesting and she fit the bill. In time, I learned she was deaf and also had multiple sclerosis. We decided that meeting would be intriguing.

She and her husband, Sam, drove the distance to come to our home. We had talked in e-mail about our communication preferences so I was confident it would be a good time. Fortunately, the sun made its appearance on this cool, September day. We chose to sit in my favorite spot where we had a bench and chairs under the huge pines with a pine needle carpet under our feet. [For Seattle folks, you realize our feet were not in mud because of the pine needles.]

When we talked, my signing came back naturally. I kept asking Karen, in sign, if she could understand my rusty signing. She assured me she could. She and my husband were able to have a wonderful conversation while Karen read Bob's lips and Bob knew how to effectively speak to someone deaf. It was a fun afternoon and I learned her story is as positive as she appeared to be in person.

Before they arrived, I picked a colander full of blackberries and made a simple cobbler to bake after they arrived. Later in the afternoon, we moved inside and savored warm cobbler with ice cream melting into a purple pool. The sweet dessert seemed to dissolve the final barriers of communication and we chattered in animated fashion. I knew eventually I would write about Karen and was thrilled when she agreed to be interviewed for my book.

KAREN CHRIEST STUELAND,
Seattle, Washington

In the Beginning . . .

Karen's maternal grandfather noticed her deafness first when she was one year old. She had been told the scenario went something like this:

"Karen, sweetie—come here," her grandfather called to her as she waddled out of the room.

No response.

"Karen, can you hear me? Come here child." he called again. His mind must have clenched like a fist when he realized Karen must not be able to hear.

He talked to her mother and she took her as quickly as she could to an Ear, Nose, and Throat specialist who referred them to an audiologist. The audiologist confirmed Karen's hearing loss was severe.

Karen and I both began life with hearing loss. She was diagnosed much younger than me and evidently had a more severe loss. One obvious difference in our early lives is that her grandfather and mother took action, without reserve, to learn first if it was true Karen could not hear well and secondly, to find what was available for her daughter. I applaud them for their actions especially since Karen and I were growing up in the fifties and sixties when technology was on the brink of discovery in the field of hearing loss. Not much could be done for us to hear better but Karen was able to sort her way into living in the hearing world with support. Many children and adults never have that. My take on Karen's early years and her family's support is that it helped her become the strong woman she is today.

My lack of support, or acknowledgement, made it harder for me to become who I am today but we did end up with similar self-confidence and joy in life. We each took different roads to get to a similar destination.

During her childhood, no one in her family used American Sign Language, including Karen. But now her sister and one brother are learning to sign with Karen and her husband, Sam.

Karen was first taught using the oral method and then total communication. That is also when she learned MCE (Manually Coded English), when she was fourteen. She learned ASL in high school but it was when she entered Gallaudet University that she was finally exposed to using ASL.

Mixed Blessings and Hassles

Karen was mainstreamed (attended a regular school rather than being sent to a school for the Deaf); part of her time was spent in the regular classroom and about 20 percent of the time was spent in a day program for the Deaf. Her mother preferred that Karen stay at home and not be sent away to a school for the Deaf. "I do not blame her. I can understand how parents want their children at home," Karen told me.

Her mainstream experience holds mixed emotions and memories. Whereas my memories seem hazy and, at times, I wonder if I remember correctly. Talking with Karen confirmed that my memories are real.

During the time she was in mainstream classes, she had no interpreter but she didn't know sign language yet. She remembers having no clue what the teachers were saying while she sat in the front row and looked at the books. She would look at what page the class was on and follow. "I just did my best. After class, I would get the summary and depend heavily on reading." In retrospect, I must have used the same tactic, minus the summary.

Keeping her positive outlook, she remembers how an annoyance became an unexpected blessing.

"One time in the eighth grade, at Wilson Middle School in Seattle in 1974," Karen told me, "a hearing boy sat behind me and kicked my desk every single day for awhile—for maybe a month or two and I patiently ignored him. Finally he stopped and we almost became best friends.

"I guess it was worth ignoring his behavior. I still remember his name—Tom Kidd. I would love to know how he is doing today," Karen said with a smile.

Cherished Communication Choices

Karen said that being deaf influenced her decision to prefer socializing with other people who are deaf instead of hearing. She felt this desire to befriend other deaf children most often during recess and lunch time. Even though she was mainstreamed in hearing classes, she loved communication and found that easiest with other deaf youth.

My recesses were filled with playing four-square, jump rope, dodge ball and flying high on the swings. Most of my classmates had

been in class with me since kindergarten, with a few new people every
year. I just played with whoever was doing the activity I liked at the
time. But I know there were no other children with hearing loss.

Karen's after-school activities were similar to mine but she had
different experiences.

"After-school activities with hearing kids, well . . . I was involved
in a musical play with the hearing kids and it went 'okay' because I
was not the only deaf kid in it. Another deaf classmate was also in the
play and we kept each other company. Ironically, one of the hearing
kids in that play became a sign language interpreter later in life. Small
world. Her name is Glenna Bain.

"One thing I did during this play is every time we (were supposed
to) sing a song, I mouthed the words, not using my voice. I do not
know if they realized what I was doing."

Karen also joined a club in high school for hearing kids but felt left
out. "I had no idea what was happening and one day I just stood up
and said, 'I do not know what is happening and I am not happy and
I am not comfortable and I feel not included' and I quit and left the
club. They did not bother to work it out with me.

"Their loss," Karen said as she shrugged her shoulders.

In high school, I thrived with music. My hearing loss must have
been mild to moderate since I was able to be in musicals and choruses
without difficulty. Girl Scouts was my only after-school activity except drama and music. Again, most of our troop knew each other
from Brownie scouts to our senior year of high school.

Karen had a few hearing friends in school. She appreciated their
efforts to communicate with her and be her friends. Those hearing
children who did befriend her went the extra mile to let Karen feel a
part of their lives.

After learning sign language, high school life changed for the better. She had a sign language interpreter and felt her world exploding.
Her thirst for knowledge was "finally quenched." Sign language is visual communication so she was able to understand 100% compared

with the research that indicates people understand only 30 percent of lip reading.

"My knowledge of the world expanded rapidly. It was so nice. And in most of my mainstreamed classes, I was not the only deaf kid mainstreaming. I had three others with me, so I was not lonely there. In the elementary and middle school, I was the only deaf kid mainstreaming most of the time. I could have had an oral interpreter but I was not aware of this possibility then," said Karen.

Thirst for Knowledge Quenched Further

Karen attended Western Oregon, Seattle, and Gallaudet universities to obtain her bachelor's degree in psychology. Then she attended Lewis and Clark College for her Master's degree in Deaf Education.

She has worked as a Professional Service Provider interpreting for Deaf-Blind persons for more than twenty years and has taught workshops and classes on deafness, ASL, Deaf culture, and more. She currently is the Director of Education at the Hearing, Speech and Deafness Center in Seattle.

Family and Siblings

Her parents, two younger brothers and sister are all hearing. "I don't think my deafness bothered them and they still included me a lot in their activities," Karen recalled.

When they were both quite young, her sister came home from school crying about a problem in her class.

"I wish we went to the same school," her sister cried.

"I know it's hard for you that I don't go to the neighborhood school with you," Karen must have said, comforting her sister. "It's hard on me, too."

She felt isolated and her siblings knew this. "My sister said to me recently she felt bad I was frustrated with communication growing up. So she felt she owes me by learning to sign now. I appreciate her," Karen said.

In the last few years, Karen learned that her family had a habit that when they talked about a topic at meal time, each of them took turns summarizing to her what they were talking about. "Also, my sister is very good at reading my lips so we would 'talk' without voicing at meals. Funny," Karen said.

Karen's mom gave her responsibilities as the oldest, despite her deafness. "She was good about letting me baby-sit my brothers and sister while she was working. She knew I could do it. My Mom and sister are good at believing I can do anything, such as appointing me to be executor of their wills," Karen said. This early trust in her abilities allowed Karen to grow into a woman who loves challenges.

Honest, Grandma, I Am Deaf—Now

Karen's brothers and sister often introduced her to their friends as "hard of hearing." She would correct them by saying she is deaf. Her maternal grandmother did the same thing. "I was puzzled why they said I was hard of hearing. I think it is because I read lips so well and I speak clearly."

When she was old enough to be curious, Karen saw copies of her audiograms from her first diagnosis. She realized she had more hearing when she was younger. "That must be why they would say I was hard of hearing, but gradually, over the years, my hearing decreased, so now I am profoundly deaf. I still hear a lot with my hearing aid in my left ear but have poor speech discrimination because of speech distortion."

Karen noticed that one of her deaf friends often asked his or her deaf friends to join them whenever they would go to family gatherings, so they would not feel left out (with no one to talk with), during family activities, reunions, and parties. "I thought, 'That is a good idea.' I did not do that while growing up in a hearing family," she said to me.

My scenario at family gatherings was different. If I lost track of the conversation, I often found myself scanning bookshelves for a book or beginning a game like pick-up-sticks or solitaire. As I grew older, I relegated myself to the kitchen to clean up so I would not need to struggle to hear. My Grandmother Page became hard of hearing in her eighties. More than once, I would sit next to her and we would just smile. One time I remember her saying, "You can't hear anything either, can you, Elizabeth?" and I nodded "No." She understood my loneliness.

Karen, the Person

"I was known to be quiet and shy when I was younger and now that I am older, I am less quiet than before, but am still quiet," Karen said smiling. "I am not a party person. Now I pretend not to be shy but inside me, I am still shy and I am good at fooling people. I tell them I am shy and they cannot believe me. I love books, cats, traveling, my marriage, being home and having my stepson Michael around.

"I am close to my family and certain friends. I'm known to be a responsible person. I'm known to be stubborn with my husband, Sam. He has a great sense of humor." Sam is late-deafened and has other physical struggles, yet he maintains a happy demeanor. He received a cochlear implant (CI) in 2005. It had to be modified for him so he could continue to have MRIs (Magnetic Resonance Imagery) and late the same year, he was able to have the CI completed so the magnet attaches firmly now.

How Others See You

Karen said when others, hearing or not, see her, she thinks they see her as a Deaf person who is a teacher, "But I think there are (people) who just see me as a deaf person and that is it. I think it depends on their attitude toward Deaf people as a whole that influences how they see me."

When I first met Karen, I knew she was deaf because we had communicated and set up a time to meet. I wanted to know more about her, and I wanted to brush up on my signing. Once she and I had visited for a few minutes, I felt I had known her for a long time. She is an easy-going, intelligent person with strong people skills.

Karen said about other people, "I think if they are open-minded, they would see me as an individual person but if they are ignorant or close-minded, then they probably see me as a Deaf person who cannot do anything or is limited."

This latter way of thinking is still prevalent in our society, but many people, like Karen, are changing the way hearing people perceive people who are Deaf. How often I have heard, "I can do everything but hear," from people born Deaf.

Karen still gets the question, "Do you drive?" which, of course, is preposterous. One time when I was giving a presentation on hearing loss and Deafness, I got this question. Later, my answer made me laugh. I said that I was a very "visual" driver. Good thing or else driving would be hazardous with me on the road. What I meant was my visual skills perk up as a deaf driver.

"I do not like it when (hearing people) ask if I can read lips. I tell them the research shows (language) is 30 percent distinguishable on the lips," Karen said. "I tell them I prefer they ask how I want to communicate. I prefer they meet me half way by trying to communicate with me instead of me going all the way to their side to communicate their way," Karen said insistently.

I related to this comment from my experiences at Holy Cross Lutheran Church of the Deaf in Columbus, Ohio. On my first visit, I was amazed at the first question each person asked. "Are you Deaf? Hearing? Which?" I would sign hard of hearing and people would sign and talk (if they normally spoke.) Then I would ask them the same question and next we shared our names. No one ever asked me if I read lips, signed, or both. They observed and we had no trouble communicating.

Karen became curious about how her co-workers saw her and how they perceived her communication needs. "I e-mailed some of my co-workers and their responses varied. One said she thinks she saw me as a co-worker who is deaf and she said she felt scared and intimidated because she was new at work and has no ability to sign, so she was embarrassed that she didn't know how to sign. She was scared about communicating with me.

"Another co-worker said she saw me first as a co-worker when introduced to me as one of the directors. Then she found out I am deaf," Karen said.

One other co-worker said she thinks she sees Karen as a co-worker first but absolutely notes her as a co-worker who is deaf. Another sees Karen as a teacher because she is aware of her job and has worked with her in education.

The answers all seemed honest and, in particular, that of her program assistant who said, "It is hard for me to answer because I know you as a person, but I am trying to be honest and think back to when I first was meeting people who are deaf. I think I saw them first as a deaf person who is a co-worker."

While the response was mixed, it helped Karen learn how she comes across to co-workers and areas she might want to improve with these same people.

Karen works in an environment where there are other deaf staff members and they provide services to Deaf and hard of hearing clients or consumers. There are two women named Karen at her work place. One friend at work talks to her family about her day and refers to the "Tall Karen" or the "Deaf Karen" when relaying stories of her day. I am guessing it's a good thing "our" Karen is not tall.

"When people get to know me a little better, they probably see me as a professional or a friend who just happened to be Deaf," Karen added.

How Do You See Hearing People?

It is only fair that we turn the tables and see how Karen perceives a hearing person upon meeting him or her.

"It depends. If I see a hearing person who happens to sign fluently, I just see a hearing signer. If I see a hearing person who does not know sign language, then I see a hearing person.

"But if I go to the doctor, I don't think he/she is hearing, I just think he/she is a doctor. If I go to my chiropractor, I do not think he is hearing, I just think of him as a chiropractor," Karen said.

Hearing People Are Better?

Karen's perception growing up in a hearing world deaf made for an interesting viewpoint. "For a very long time, I always thought hearing people are better than deaf people. And that hearing people know more than deaf people.

"Now I know it is not true at all. My self-esteem started to increase. Now I tell people that some Deaf people may *appear* to know less, but it is not because of intelligence. It is because of communication barriers." Many deaf people are not exposed to the same type of interactions as hearing peers. Karen explained that while growing up, deaf people miss out on a lot of incidental knowledge.

A typical example would be at the dinner table when hearing parents talk about what is happening in their work places and hearing siblings listen to the conversation and learn while listening. "Whereas, deaf children do not have access to that auditory conversation and miss the opportunity to learn about the work world."

When Karen was young, she remembers thinking hearing people were perfect. "But later I realized they are human just like us with flaws, faults, issues, etc. Boy, was I naïve."

"Oh, Never Mind"

A common frustration Deaf and hard of hearing people share is when a hearing person is talking and realizes we did not "get it;" he or she will say "Never mind" or "It's not important," or say less to us than if we were hearing.

"I. King Jordan said it best when he stated 'Deaf people can do anything except hear.' That is what I would like the hearing world to know," Karen said meaning it.

"My husband, who is late-deafened, had surgery and was in the hospital for four days. I was amazed with the nurses there. I told them I wanted to show them some basic signs and they agreed to learn and used them beautifully whenever they came in and communicated with my husband in his hospital room. They could ask if he wanted more medicine for pain, ask if he was hungry or wanted water. And these same nurses were great at accepting an interpreter when discussing things at a high level of discretion," Karen recalled.

Etiquette

Hearing people often will stare when seeing people use sign language. A friend of mine asked me once why hearing people gawk at her when she signs. Knowing it bothers Deaf people, I asked Karen for her reaction.

"It depends. If hearing people know sign language or are learning sign language and do not inform us, that would be rude because we thought we were having a private conversation. If hearing people are innocent and watch us out of healthy curiosity and are not aware of the culture rule, that is fine but I might be self-conscious anyway," Karen responded. The other side of the coin is if hearing people watch Deaf people signing and make fun or mock the actions. What would Karen do if she saw this happening?

"I would not like that at all and might comment by educating them. I might ignore. It depends on my mood. One time I was traveling on a train with my husband, Sam, and we sat at a table for a meal with a father and his son.

"His son appeared to talk about us by putting the menu in front of his face and turned toward his father. I got mad and told the boy it is very rude and that we are very normal deaf people who are educated and can do anything. Some kids often asked 'Are we death?' Geez," Karen remarks.

Involvement and Goals

Karen said her involvement in Deaf culture is more in the Deaf-Blind world. "I have some close friends who are Deaf and I do attend some Deaf-related community events. I am more involved in the Deaf-Blind world by having Deaf-Blind friends, interpreting for Deaf-Blind people, being on the board for the Deaf-Blind Service Center and my volunteering.

"In the hearing world, I joined the MS chat room (on www .msworld.org) for people with MS online and I have a hearing family. I have some hearing friends who are signers, too," Karen shared.

Karen's personal goal, other than living a full and active life, involves one of her strongest talents—bridging the gap between the Deaf and hearing worlds. "I want to bridge the communication gap between hearing people or interpreters and late-deafened people who learn ASL later in life, or deaf people who were deprived of communication while growing up. I want to do this by clarifying communication and enlightening them on how to communicate more effectively," Karen said with passion.

Dreams

Her life dreams have been fulfilled throughout her forty-eight years of life so far. "A lot of my dreams of traveling around the United States, traveling in Europe for six months, to India and Nepal, owning a home and being married have been filled already. Also, I am blessed to have a stepson. I do want to be married for a long time to my husband, Sam. One dream, to remain mobile in spite of my disease, MS, is yet to be fulfilled," Karen added, knowing I understood.

Something tells me that Karen will do whatever she needs to do to see that her life stays open and full. I feel proud and happy to have met her and to know there are people like Karen in this life.

CAITLIN, Upstate New York

Caitlin, eighteen, leads an active life as a teen. She faces many of the typical challenges every young person faces, but they are magnified by her deafness. Caitlin has worn hearing aids since she was five and her hearing has progressively become worse. "My mom said a Cochlear Implant is an option for me. I might decide to get one someday," she said.

Caitlin's mother, Carol, said that Caitlin's hearing loss was discovered at age four when she took her to an ENT to be evaluated. Caitlin was still not talking. "She was labeled speech delayed," Carol said, sounding weary about the memory of it. "They didn't find her hearing loss until she began kindergarten and was in speech and occupational therapy. They told us she would be in it for the long term." The speech therapist told Carol and Steve that Caitlin had hearing loss.

"Caitlin was a stubborn child and didn't like the testing. It took several times to get the test right," Carol remembered. Caitlin started wearing hearing aids that same year. "Caitlin always knew she needed them and wore them. They were, and still are, the first thing she puts on in the morning and the last thing to do at night. [Taking them off.] She was never embarrassed about hearing aids and never covered them up." This teen has various colored ear molds and since pink is her favorite color, that is her choice at the moment. The different colored ear molds were just coming into existence, as far as I know, in the late nineties so I never opted to get them. I always kept my hair cut above my ears and even with the hearing aids visible, most people never saw them. But I do remember one young teen at Holy Cross Lutheran Church for the Deaf who showed me her different ear molds on Sundays. It was a way for us to connect and share a chuckle.

Not Only Kids Can Be Cruel

"In elementary school, teachers would say 'Caitlin is way into your face,'" Carol remembered. "She was young and no one understood that being a lip reader, she has to be close to see. Face to face. I would try to explain and they didn't understand."

"The teachers would say, 'the kids don't like her.' It was hard to advocate for her to even have a seat in front of the class," Carol said.

The teachers finally moved her up front when her school speech therapist went to bat for her needs.

"I used to have a really hard time in school. I got picked on constantly and everyone kept saying how I am deaf and dumb and [called me horrible] other names. I had a horrible time from second grade to tenth grade," Caitlin said. "No one would be friends with me because I am 'different.'" The name calling increased and other students decided they could push her around as well. "They wrote notes about me and they eventually came to me so I knew what they said. They wrote that deaf people are worthless and that I should be with the retards. I came home almost every night crying because I was so upset," Caitlin said while remembering. "My teachers didn't care about helping me out more; they didn't understand my hearing loss."

Caitlin has an FM Listening system, where the teacher, or speaker, wears a tiny microphone and pager-sized device, and the person with hearing loss has the receiver attached to a hearing aid. It takes the speaker's voice directly to the student, improving comprehension. Some of her teachers refused to wear the microphone. "Two teachers even made a point of wearing it and not even turning it on," Carol told me. When this took place, Caitlin thought something was wrong with her hearing aids. I have used this FM system in the workplace, church and social places, when I was wearing hearing aids, and at least I knew the topic, making conversation somewhat less stressful. Why teachers would refuse to help a student in this simple way is beyond my understanding. What a waste.

By the time she was a sophomore, Caitlin felt some of the teachers were agonizingly unkind, making class time more difficult. As any teacher will explain, students tend to lean their heads on their hands, as if they could hear better this way. I remember doing this and Caitlin was no exception to this rule.

But when Caitlin did this, her hearing aids squealed. She could not hear the sound and her teachers did not hesitate to tell her to move her hand. "Teachers would throw a paper clip at my hand by my ear. Classes were eighty minutes long and teachers did it to get me out of the habit. [These same] teachers made a rule that you *could* lean on your hand if you did not wear hearing aids. I want people to know [this happens]," said Caitlin. The "paper clip teacher" said that Caitlin was taking advantage of being different.

"My teachers kinda took advantage of *me*. As it turns out, my hearing aids weren't really squealing half the time. [One time] I got kicked out of the room because my hearing aids were squealing. Then when I tried going back in the classroom, they locked me out! That was when I had enough. The kids and the teachers hated me—all because I am deaf," Caitlin concluded.

The embarrassment was often more than she could bear. Hopefully, the other students and teachers didn't really hate Caitlin, but these emotions of hers are real and valid. Whether or not they did, she felt they did. So often people with any special need are misunderstood, abused and ostracized.

Mom and Dad

Caitlin's parents were her sole support. When they learned of the teachers' refusal to assist their daughter, her mom, Carol, said she had nights she could not sleep because of the way Caitlin was being treated. These two teachers refused to go out of the way to help her. "She was failing in school and said things like, 'I guess I am dumb' and we knew we needed to get her help. The real problem started in 10th grade with academics. The peer problems started in fourth grade when they wouldn't play with her and taunted her and she had no friends, so we knew something had to be done," Carol said.

Carol and Steve took an action they never dreamt they would need to do. They filed a formal complaint with the school. The complaint is still in the courts.

Her parents get the feeling from others in town that they are doing something horrible. But they are doing it out of love for their daughter and so, hopefully, it won't happen to any other children. "It has been a hard time for us but especially for Caitlin. She had to testify in court and it was very emotional for her."

The more the school delved into the complaint, the more disturbed they were with the behavior of the now-removed teachers. They refused to write assignments on the board or have a note taker, or allow classmates to help Caitlin. The example of their cruelty was passed on to classmates, showing them how NOT to treat other people. "I wonder about what other kids do when their parents won't fight for them?" Carol mused.

"She was a very unhappy child before and we knew why. It wasn't easy to deal with her because she was unhappy all the time. She is very social and was withdrawn. I think the time I *really* understood (what Caitlin was hearing) was when I walked into the family room and the television volume was very low. It clicked in that this is what Caitlin's day is like," Carol remembered.

Time for a Drastic Change

The best choice they discovered, for Caitlin's new school, was the Board of Cooperative Educational Services (BOCES), which is a career and technical high school. Carol said students attend BOCES because they didn't do well in regular schools. This high school offers teachers who accept students' needs and classes are small.

Carol said she can talk with these high school teachers, now that her daughter is in a new school. "Caitlin has changed. She is a teen-aged girl."

In Summer 2007, Caitlin attended Career Exploration camp at the National Technical Institute of the Deaf (NTID). She tested so well that the administrators wanted to talk to her parents, but they were not aware of this until they took the three-hour drive home. "We'll definitely make the trip back to NTID soon," Carol exclaimed. At this camp, Caitlin met kids from all over the United States and every class used open captioning, ASL and speakers.

At Caitlin's current school, the teachers go out of their way to get what she needs, including an interpreter and a note taker. The suggestions keep coming in to make things easier for Caitlin, and she is thriving.

Caitlin has a brother, Jason, twenty-five. "He understands Caitlin cannot hear. But sometimes we do get impatient." They did the typical things to have her hear better—facing her, speaking normally, and so on. "We knew we couldn't holler from another room. People need to look right at people with hearing loss to communicate," Carol said.

"Caitlin is stronger. She is herself and has no problem being herself," said her mom, smiling. Her interests keep blossoming and she keeps right on pushing the envelope to learn and do more.

Life Is Good Now

"All the kids treat me so much better. They learned sign so they can communicate with me. My teachers are awesome. They write stuff on the board and they even e-mail me on what they did in class," said a contented Caitlin.

"I am getting good grades and I am getting an interpreter soon. I can't wait 'til that happens. So basically—life is good now." She pushes herself to excel in everything. Her junior year she was inducted into the National Technical Honor Society with an average of 94 percent. She has learned to use clay to make bowls and went to Odyssey of the Mind to help sell them. This was all volunteer work that earned her a trip to Dorney Amusement Park.

Caitlin is an avid reader. As she learns ASL, having begun in tenth grade, she has noticed her English writing and speech is changing. This year, she had to take an English test to evaluate writing skills. She thinks she did poorly.

"I don't think my writing is that great. I don't exactly write like a hearing person, and I don't really know how."

Differences

For readers who have no knowledge of American Sign Language, it is important for you to know that ASL and English are two separate languages. ASL is not a re-configuration of English. When I learned ASL, I noted how many extraneous words we often use in English to make the same point as ASL.

Also, note that for Deaf people who use ASL, English is their second language. They think in ASL. I found, after a period of time learning ASL that I often think in sign, especially when it comes to songs and prayers.

Another Challenge

Caitlin has plenty of energy. She played volleyball at her new school her junior year and literally threw herself into the game. Maybe she worked so hard to compensate for her hearing aids not working well in the gym during the active practices and games. She told me that her hearing aids didn't fall off but they were affected by the gym lights. More frustrating for her, though, was the fact she could not hear her teammates call to her. She opted out of playing volleyball the following year.

Her four years of sports was called finished by Caitlin. "It makes me sad but I couldn't hear my teammates when they 'got it' and I ran into them a couple of times," she said with a sigh. "It has taken a huge toll on me. My teammates were frustrated—and so was I. I tried *really* hard. I didn't know what else to do."

Moving on

At the youthful age of eighteen, Caitlin has already experienced ridicule, growing pains, learning obstacles, triumph, exclusion and inclusion and a gradual loss of hearing. Yet her family has stood by her, even when they could not understand her silent world. Her parents believe she is stronger for her adversity and are proud of the strides she takes daily to persevere.

Her hearing peers also live through much of what she has experienced—yet deafness has been a catalyst for Caitlin to try harder, prove herself and learn how to do her best.

This young woman has many chapters yet to live in her life. I want to think of her as a smiling adult who finds contentment without limitations. One who will look back on her life with the satisfaction that deafness never persuaded her to quit.

I would like to write that story, too.

ANTHONY, Texas

"Like my mother said, I was three when they found out," Anthony, now thirty-nine, remembered. The stories of his hearing loss discovery are confusing for him. "My father thinks I was eighteen months old, [so I am] not sure anymore. [There is] no proof, [and the] cause is unknown. No one else in my family was deaf; I am an only child. Two of my three children are deaf, so I think I must have been born deaf. Anne, my wife, is hearing."

Anthony grew up in the Seattle area and was born deaf into a hearing family but his parents have conflicting stories.

"I remember my mother saying I went to the doctor and was checked out and the doctor said I was deaf. He suggested to my parents that they send me to a residential Deaf school but they didn't want me to go there.

"My feeling is that mom didn't want me to be far away or she didn't want me to be seen as handicapped or lesser. Also, I suspect that my mother feels guilty for doing something wrong which caused my deafness. She still tries to deny me being Deaf and wanted me to be oral and attend an oral program.

"My father told me that he did try to tell my mother that I should go to a signing school but my mother refused. They argued a lot over me." Parents' arguing is difficult for any child, for any reason, but to know your parents are arguing over you would make the pain personal and devastating.

Mainstreamed/Oral

He spent his school days mainstreamed beginning with an oral, public preschool from age three to five. Next was Bowlake Elementary School where he was partially mainstreamed from grades one through three.

From age ten to thirteen, he attended St. Joseph's Institute for the Deaf in Missouri which is a private, oral, residential school.

Anthony remembers what it was like being away from home.

"All of the teachers were nuns. At the beginning I was afraid, yes, it was so far away. Then I got used to it and had great fun with many friends. All of the students never used sign language at St. Joseph's. We all lip read and spoke. The teachers did the same."

Many hearing parents with Deaf children may not understand the emotional need for their children to have a peer group in the Deaf community. During Anthony's childhood, these issues still were not discussed openly, as they are today. The oral schools taught children to read lips and use their own voice as a form of communication, hoping they would work and live in the hearing world. These same children have never heard their voice and talk by feel and imitation. The schools that taught sign language relied solely on signing, which includes many facial and body language movements. Using sign is not the way to integrate into the hearing world, especially if no other communication skills are utilized. So the conflict continues today; which is the best way for your child?

"I had never seen sign language before in my life. How did I feel about being far away? I felt nothing, didn't miss them. I was active at school with homework, classes, activities, friends, sports, etc. I got in some trouble at times; the teachers were very strict.

"Most of the teachers worked one-on-one with students to communicate. If a teacher didn't understand what I was saying, then she wouldn't give me any points. High points earned trips to get ice cream or fun stuff. I had to work hard on my speech to get points and do the fun stuff.

"If not, I couldn't go. I'd stay home (at school) and be bored by myself. During school, each classroom had a system with a microphone on the desk. We wore head phones. During class, if someone spoke, they needed to use the microphone so others could hear. It was so much work to catch what was being said. [It was] a lot of work for my ears to try and listen. Now, my opinion is that I was not successful. I am profoundly deaf and struggled a lot then," he said.

To Sign or Not to Sign

By grade seven, Anthony was back in Washington attending Highland Middle School where he was again partially mainstreamed and learned Signed English in this public school. He entered a self-contained classroom of deaf students. He was overwhelmed because everyone signed and he didn't understand and felt completely lost. He had no knowledge of signing.

The teacher used Total Communication and Anthony could lip read pretty well. The teacher signed for the deaf students and he could lip read enough. A few months after entering school, the teacher assigned a book report. The deaf students used sign to present their reports and the teacher interpreted in English orally so he could try and read her lips. When it was his turn, the teacher signed while he spoke his report orally. After this incident, the teacher said she felt it was too much for her being in between the signing deaf students and Anthony and asked him if he wanted to learn Signed English. He agreed readily and was eager and happy to learn.

After school, he was excited and went home to tell his mom what the teacher said about beginning to learn to sign at school. "My mother was very mad and bawled me out. 'You won't use sign. You can lip read and speak, you will be fine.' So I told her I'd keep being oral.

"The next day, I went to school and told my teacher that I was ready to learn how to sign. So I hid it from my mother and learned without her knowing. I increased my knowledge quickly. Mom never knew until about two years later when a very good friend of mine, who was deaf, wanted to stay the night at my house.

"He came over and we began to sign together in my bedroom. My mother happened to see us signing together then mom came up to me immediately and said, 'Why are you signing? How do you know?' I said, 'He is deaf and can't lip read. He doesn't understand. I must sign with him.' Then mom said nothing and let it go," Anthony concluded.

He moved to Ohio when he was sixteen; there he attended Hilliard High School near Columbus. Anthony was fully mainstreamed with no signing, no interpreter and some tutoring. Anthony talked candidly about his day-to-day life in school throughout his childhood.

"It was really bad because I didn't know anything about Deaf culture or Sign Language until I was 13. (What he learned was Signed English, not ASL. When he was 19 he learned ASL.) I thought that all deaf people were oral. When I began school, I felt like I didn't know any better. I just went through school," he recalled.

"At thirteen years of age, I was confused because I met deaf students who used Signed English and I didn't understand them. I finally learned to sign and wished I had learned long before that. My mother always forced me to attend an oral school and didn't want me to sign at all; she wanted to avoid signing completely."

Today these memories are still clear and are difficult to think about for any length of time. "Right now, my feeling is that my past was really an awful experience, but I can't believe that I got through it. I graduated high school, I got a diploma, I attended college, now I have a great job; I am lucky."

In his final two years of high school, Anthony attended Tolles Technical School in Plain City, Ohio, learning design and drafting and he had no interpreter. This would lead to his career.

"Lucky I didn't get lost or too behind in my education. I tried to socialize with others in the mainstream who couldn't sign. We would rarely write. I often felt lonely, but if there was a deaf student there, we would chat and enjoy each other.

"I believe that God was really watching over me and helped me growing up. God is an important part of my life now," Anthony added, but not as an afterthought.

Isolation is all too common for children who are deaf and raised orally in a hearing family. Anthony was no exception. Yet this fact does not help sweeten the sour memories of feeling alone. This feeling of isolation can carry into our adult world if we must work in the hearing environment.

"All growing up I felt isolated. I had no real friends or skills to make many new friends. It was hard to communicate with hearing people and I felt left out. Now I feel isolated while I work because no one signs and there is no interpreter there. People focus on their work."

Family—Then and Now

His parents have never signed at all and still don't. "Mostly they spoke to me and I voiced growing up. But now I feel uncomfortable speaking with them."

He had many bad experiences while growing up, especially when it came to family gatherings where extended family was present.

"At Thanksgiving dinner, [I] was very bitter because I saw everyone talking all over the place and no one ever talked to me. So, I simply ate my food, finished, watched TV or played outside alone," Anthony recalled.

Anthony broke this cycle of exclusion with his wife and children. "Right now I do not feel so alone or isolated with my own family because I have two daughters who are Deaf and my wife and son sign. We enjoy time together. When we all visit my family, it is the same problem as it was growing up.

"No one signs and they always talk directly to my wife instead of talking to me. They take advantage of my wife who signs. I hate to see her in the middle of me and my family. I know that my wife (Anne) gets frustrated with them because they can't communicate with me at all—then or now."

The fact that Anthony has had this personal pain in his own family breaks Anne's heart, and she is frustrated that his parents never tried to learn who their son was. Even today, they don't try at all, which makes no sense to her. "It makes me so sad when we get together with his family. They are missing out on so much. ASL is such an expressive language, and so much is lost in the interpretation. I feel like his family will never know Anthony and our daughters directly. They are only getting a part of them," Anne said with tears filling her eyes.

"I resent them not learning to sign. I think it's abusive what his parents put him through," she said scowling. "I get angry that they continue to deny that he prefers American Sign Language and it's most effective for him. They control him still in some ways. I try and avoid gatherings with his family because I 'work' a lot (interpreting), and my family gets bored and restless.

"Interactions are very superficial with his family. There's no real connection," Anne said. It's not just Anne and Anthony who feel this. The children feel it, see it and swallow the feelings and isolation they see from their grandparents. The visits tire the family but pull them together as a core group. "Because of his upbringing and the choices his family made, Anthony feels so behind in English now, as an adult, and feels he may never 'catch up.' He struggles with self-esteem in the hearing world and feels not fluent enough in ASL because of learning it so late in life.

"He wished he had grown up signing in a Deaf school and knew Deaf children and adults. He didn't meet his first Deaf adult until he was like twenty. That's terrible," Anne said. "Our daughters are so advanced and intelligent and beautiful communicators. Anthony is proud of them and we are proud that we have given them such a strong foundation in ASL and they are now mastering English as a second language." My guess is their daughters agree and see the pain in their parent's eyes when at these family gatherings. Fortunately, they did not have to live through this same nightmare and respect their parents all the more for their choices.

Maybe Anthony's parents didn't want to make the extra effort. It's a hard nut to crack when those who are supposed to love us refuse to meet us even part way. This pain never leaves.

ASL Its Own True Language

Real communication takes real effort on each person's part. It is equally important for hearing and Deaf people to seek solutions. People who are Deaf and use ASL are also called native signers, as opposed to those who prefer to speak first and sign second.

Sentence structure in ASL is *not* simplified English, as some people might have learned or conjectured, including me. Anthony's wife, Anne, offers the clearest explanation I have seen or heard in years. This clarifies how important it is to know that ASL is a true language.

"When you compare ASL to English, it makes it sound like ASL is somehow related to English or derived from English or a primitive or inferior language. Much research proves that ASL is as complex and complete as any spoken language, that it evolved separately from spoken language and has all the ingredients of a bona fide language. It is simply its own language. Nothing is deleted or left out. Use of space, body, facial expressions, role shifting, nonmanual markers, etc., conveys all the necessary subtleties that English or any other language conveys. The grammar, vocabulary, semantics, rules, and all the properties of a language exist in ASL and they are distinct and separate from English. This holds true for any other foreign spoken language and foreign signed language around the world."

Some colleges are accepting ASL as a foreign language for college credits.

Writing can be an option for communication based on the Deaf person's knowledge of English. For a deaf person who prefers ASL, an interpreter is a much better choice. It is crucial during such events as job interviews or doctor's office visits.

On the same note, writing to a hearing person will come out different than standard English format and can be confusing to the hearing person. If each person maintains patience and a willingness to communicate, this should never be an obstacle. Embarrassment is common when Deaf people realize their writing does not match hearing people's perception of English. I have seen this same reaction in people from other countries who are hesitant to speak or write in English.

Eye contact is very important to Deaf people. "When I look at hearing people, they are offended or uncomfortable, but this is a way that I understand their emotions and what they feel. I must look at them. Deaf people value visual communication," Anthony said.

Learning basic signs can be done by a visit to the library. There are many books on basic sign where one can learn fingerspelling and simple signs such as, "my name is," "can I help you?" and similar phrases. Any effort to communicate in any sign will help bridge the gap between hearing and Deaf people.

"Hearing people should know that Deaf people have very expressive faces; that is part of their language, ASL. (Many) hearing people move their lips and have very straight faces, but Deaf people are very expressive. Deaf people don't always have clear speech.

"Growing up, I called myself hard of hearing. I used my voice, lip read, I wore hearing aids. But I was lost," Anthony said, meaning it.

When he was nineteen, he finally called himself Deaf. "Oftentimes people encourage deaf children to call themselves hard of hearing and be in the hearing world. This isn't always right for every deaf child. I was 'hard of hearing' because I never saw ASL or met Deaf people or knew about the Deaf culture. When I got older, I met Deaf people who used ASL and had Deaf culture.

"That made me more comfortable and I felt like I fit. I no longer had to work in the hearing world and I could communicate freely with Deaf people."

No Longer Alone

Anthony talked openly about his feelings about having Deaf children.

"When my daughter was born and we found out she was deaf, I was so thrilled and had a great big smile. I felt so blessed and relieved because I was no longer alone and the only one deaf like a 'black sheep.' Now we have another daughter who is deaf and it's another blessing. My goal now is to not let my daughters go through what I went through growing up.

"I wanted them to have ASL as a first language and they do. Their second language is English. Our third child, our son, is hearing. I'm still happy and thrilled. I'm not disappointed that he's not deaf. I feel we have a great balance in our family.

"When the five of us are together, we always use ASL, not speech, and sign. Sometimes my wife voices with my son (and signs), and my son understands my voice, which I think is important."

Advice for Hearing Parents with Deaf Children

First and foremost, Anthony said parents should learn how to sign. Decisions about their children should be led by the children's needs and wishes.

"If they make one decision and it's not successful, they should change the school and not let the child suffer so long. They need to make a change. I wasn't happy and didn't have friends. I know a couple who sent their daughter to an oral school all through middle school. "Then the daughter became unhappy. Recently, for high school, they just transferred her to the Deaf school and she is happy now. I think they did what is best for their daughter—and they are Deaf themselves."

It is important that parents give deaf children experience and exposure to Deaf culture, such as Deaf clubs, a Deaf church and events in the Deaf community.

Friends—Then and Now

Most of us realize that youthful friendships help shape our self-image and how we see ourselves. Being deaf and not knowing what resources are available would make for a lonely childhood.

There are very few ASL idioms—one of them is "touch finish" which means "been there" in English, while "never touch" means "never been there or never experienced that" in English. I asked Anthony about clubs and he replied, "I never touched a Deaf club with Deaf people until after I had graduated from high school. Growing up I had very, very few hearing friends. Mostly none. All of them didn't know how to sign. We used writing and I would voice and lip read.

"I had a few very good deaf oral friends but they didn't live near me, they lived far away. I didn't see them outside of school," Anthony said.

Now that Anthony has learned of Deaf culture activities, he has taken part in some. "I played on the Deaf club's softball and volleyball teams. We traveled to other states to play against other Deaf clubs. Now with three kids, I don't do that anymore."

After high school, he attended Columbus Technical Institute (now Columbus State Community College) in Columbus, Ohio, for one year. He studied architecture and had an interpreter. Next, he attended The Ohio State University in Columbus for one year and continued his studies of architecture in an advanced setting and had an interpreter. It was at CTI/CSCC that Anthony finally learned ASL and more about Deaf culture.

For twenty years, Anthony has been a successful CAD (Computer Aided Design) draftsman. His desire to learn something new may propel him to a different career but for now he continues on day by day.

Anthony went to the DeaFair in October 2006. "I had a booth for my own printmaking and graphic design business. The DeaFair is an expo of anyone who signs or is Deaf or has a business, agency or organization related to deafness. I saw many different exhibits, like the relay service, interpreting agencies, and arts and crafts," Anthony told me. Anthony shared his other activities. "We have had a Deaf/Hearing Bible study group where we require 'no voicing'— everyone, Deaf or hearing, signs.

"Sometimes we go to a Deaf church. We have traveled to Deaf events. We went to the Deaf School (Ohio School for the Deaf) for their holiday play and performance. We often go to parties with Deaf people from the community."

People I have met who are born deaf have told me they need the connection with Deaf culture to feel a part of society. Isolation should not be a problem today with so many options for people who are Deaf/deaf which were foreign a few decades ago.

Since I became deaf, it is different for me—and others in my situation. Yet we can still feel this isolation in the hearing world because we, too, don't feel a part. The Internet has brought many people together around the world in chat rooms for Deaf organizations.

Anthony and his family go to arts and crafts shows and fairs that involve interaction with the hearing world. He sometimes meets hearing friends and attends open captioned movies.

"Of course my parents are in the hearing world, and I see them sometimes."

Dreams Do Come True

"I am a father, husband, and small business owner: printmaking and graphic design. Related to deafness, I am really happy that I am a member of the Deaf club and have been a member of a Deaf church because I can work with them or help them and have a good time with them," he said.

He enjoys art, camping, sports, traveling, woodworking and his puppy, Rocky, and cat, Newt.

"I enjoy spending time with my kids and my pets—I have never had a trained hearing dog, but my other dog, Missi, understood some basic signs. She passed away."

His strongest talent is creative design and art, and he is a self-proclaimed computer whiz. Anthony likes to work with his hands in carpentry, woodworking, furniture design and building. He enjoys Internet research on different topics of interest and his talents are all visual, he said.

"When I was little, I dreamt of becoming an NBA player, a policeman and an engineer. I have become an architectural draftsman (engineer), so with that [dream] I'm successful. I dreamed of owning my own business and I recently set it up. I dream of growing my business larger. I dream of retiring."

Business

Most of Anthony's art pieces incorporate ASL or the Deaf experience in some way. "I hope that Deaf people enjoy my art and that it will inspire a sense of acceptance and pride in being Deaf." He also hopes that the general (hearing) population will learn to appreciate the art of Deaf individuals, increase their level of awareness of deaf people, and gain a respect for the language and culture of the Deaf community.

He has made twelve different designs of greeting cards, woodcut and linoleum cut prints, posters and computer- and photographic-generated art. He plans to add wood sculpture, clay and glass designs as well as screen printing for shirts in the future.

Advice for Deaf Youth

Anthony would love to spare at least one youth from the lonesome childhood he experienced. Communication is the key, but it's not always simple or effective.

"If you are not happy because your parents don't sign, you have to be patient until you grow up and are independent. You can tell your parents that you want to go to a Deaf church or club or camp or whatever because you are curious and want to be around other Deaf people.

"It's easier for me to advise (hearing) parents. They can better help and influence their deaf children."

How Others See You

Anthony said that when hearing people meet him for the first time, he believes they feel awkward when they find out he is Deaf.

"They didn't realize, and they don't know how to communicate with me. For example, if someone walks up to me and talks, I gesture that I can't hear, and they feel awkward and don't know what to do. They usually give up or try to gesture with me."

He believes people see his deafness first, not the person he really is. "It's funny because if someone is talking to me but I don't realize it, they get upset and get my attention. They are upset because they think I have been ignoring them."

This is embarrassing and often the Deaf person can read the body language of the hearing person. What he or she sees can be confusing. Some hearing people seem angry because they think you were ignoring them—not understanding you hear nothing. "Sometimes if they are rude to me because I can't hear, I'll sign. Then they have no idea what I'm saying and I, in a way, am rude back to them because they don't understand sign language."

Writing messages is another way for hearing people to communicate with a person who is Deaf. Anthony has tried asking hearing people to write and some refuse. "I get mad when they refuse. They just keep talking and I don't know what they are saying.

"So I go ahead and sign and they have no idea. I've seen some positive attitudes, folks getting paper and pencil quickly and being very willing to write with me. Some know how to fingerspell and will spell words to me and are nice about it."

Overhearing Sign Language

A true contention in Deaf culture is when hearing people stare while others use sign language. The reaction of the people who are Deaf is mixed.

"Many times people stare or watch us while we are signing, but some of us notice their stares and think it's a little rude. We ignore them and continue with our meal or socializing.

"If someone comes over and says they enjoy watching our signing and ask where they can learn to sign, that is great. We are impressed with that. Many people look at us, but I am able to ignore them and continue signing; it doesn't really bother me.

"Also, sometimes we have to be careful because others may know how to sign. We have to watch what we say in public. Recently four of us went out to eat. We all sign. We heard there was another group of Deaf people coming to the restaurant and we told the waitress we didn't want to be in the same room with them because they could see our conversations. We have to watch that sometimes."

Marriage Vows Become a Reality

In 1976, we became a family of two, plus a Siamese cat, when my daughter, Mary, was two. Her father and I were married almost six years. I was young and had grown up in a small town while he had been raised in Washington, D.C., and had completed a tour of duty in the U.S. Navy which included Vietnam. Our thinking and life viewpoints were worlds apart. There never seemed to be a way to meld into a close couple. But our daughter was, and is, our joy and the one thing we always agree on.

In 2002, we had a long conversation which healed the past. We have both forgiven and moved on. Even so, in 1977, I desperately tried to give Mary a secure life and she was my whole world during this period. We now refer to this period of our lives as our macaroni and cheese and hot dog days. Mary and I moved into my Grandmother Page's [whom we affectionately called Kaki] home during this time, paying her utility bills and keeping the house for her while she was in a nursing home. I was ever mindful to walk gingerly and keep sticky fingers far from grandma's antique furniture and Steinway grand piano. I was surrounded here by a needed sense of familiarity and belonging.

My friend, Rosemary, was in the bell choir at the Church of Messiah United Methodist in Westerville, where I was still singing in the choir. She, too, was a single Mom and invited me to a single parent's meeting. At first I balked, but finally relented. I left Mary with a baby sitter and set out for Rosemary's home the next Friday evening. I got lost, went home, sent the sitter home, and called Rosemary. You need to know that I could get lost driving anywhere new and had no sense of direction back in those days.

"I can't find your home," I said to Rosemary on the phone. Knowing me, I was already planning on changing back into more comfortable clothes.

"Get the sitter back. I'll be there in five minutes," Rosemary said with the authority only a registered nurse could emit.

I had withdrawn socially and wondered why I'd ever agreed to attend this meeting. I had taken forever in deciding what to wear because my choices were few. I'd finally decided to wear a yellow polo shirt, a blue jean skirt, and a tan, suede jacket with a tie belt. I sported a Dorothy Hamill wedge haircut and no makeup. My twenty-four-year-old, freckled face was there for all to see.

Rosemary and I walked down a few steps into the meeting room. People were milling around arranging and helping themselves to refreshments. I saw the semi-circle of metal chairs and sought one out. Then, I saw him.

He was the cutest guy I'd ever seen; he wore a green leisure suit and a broad smile. His eyes were a deep blue and his smile made my mouth go dry. My heart still flutters when I remember that moment. I sat as far from him as possible because my knees were shaking uncontrollably, reflecting my nervousness.

This man sat on a chair next to me and said, "Hi, I'm Bob Thompson. What's your name?" Those who know me may not believe that I became incredibly shy and quiet.

"What was wrong with me?" I thought.

"Say your name," I kept thinking to myself at the time.

"Liz Darby," I finally managed.

He kept talking and talking while I just sat there with sweating palms and a heart and stomach that were doing an Irish jig. I kept telling myself that he was just being nice and he was not really interested in me. But my body was still doing the internal dance.

Finally, Duane Smith, the pastor, began the meeting. Bob stayed right next to me. We discussed our dreams for what we wanted to do with our lives. There were only about twelve people there that night, and everyone was asked to talk about their dreams.

Mine were all too real to speak of—I wanted to survive long enough to see my daughter grow up, I wanted to be able to pay the bills and put food on the table. My imagination kicked in and I said the most incredible things to these strangers.

"I want to be a singer," I said. "Boy, did that sound childish," I thought. I might as well have said that I wanted to be a ballerina. I don't remember what I said after that. Afterward, we went out to dinner. I rode in Rosemary's car and I'm sure she asked me what I thought about the group, but I don't remember thinking about anything else other than Bob's face and my dim-witted dream.

We arrived at Schmidt's Sausage Haus and walked across the cobblestone street to join the group. Guess who sat next to me again? Right. Bob. Rosemary and Bob knew everyone and worked to draw me into the conversation. I honestly didn't remember anything until later. But I remember that Bob kept trying to buy me something to eat or drink, but I stuck with water. In those days, money was elusive and I only carried a quarter so I could make a phone call. Then, I escaped to the restroom.

I returned to laughter and saw that people were wiping up something that had spilled. It had been Bob's beer and once it was all dry, we sat back down at the table.

"What happened?" I managed to ask.

"Oh, I'm blind in one eye and I missed the table when I set my mug down," Bob said chuckling.

"Oh sure," I said, "I think it probably means you had too much to drink." I couldn't believe I said that—where had that come from?

"No, really—I'm blind in one eye and I've only had this one beer," Bob said, laughing.

I continued to tease him, glad we actually were engaged in something resembling a conversation. His blue eyes were dancing as he searched my face in an effort to know me better. My knees remained weak and I almost couldn't stand up.

The crowd slowly thinned as the evening became morning. Rosemary was also having a great time, and she suggested later that we go to another restaurant, Max and Irma's, for dessert. Four of us were left—Rosemary, Bob, Fred, and I. What was I to do? As we walked out the door, Bob took me in his arms and twirled me in a polka dance on the street. "No," I thought, "I can't dance, plus I don't want you to feel my chubbiness."

But he couldn't hear my thoughts.

"How can we be in German Village and not do the polka?!" he exclaimed.

I was a goner at that point.

So we went toward Fred's big four-door sedan and Bob gently nudged me to sit in the back seat with him. He put his arm around my shoulder and brushed his lips against mine.

"I'd like your phone number, Liz," he said as I caught my breath.

"Sure, I'll write it down at the restaurant," I gasped, trying to sound normal.

Even after all the German food Bob had already eaten, he ordered a garbage burger at Max and Irma's. He was [and is] not a big guy.

He asked me again if he could buy me something to eat and I looked at the menu for the least expensive item. I selected a 50-cent dish of ice cream and I picked at it until it melted. We parted company around 1:30 A.M., and I was lost in my thoughts all the way home. I knew I was smitten and Rosemary knew it, too. I never dreamt he would ever call or see me again because I had low self-esteem at the time. Again, I was proven wrong. I can still smell the night air on that April Fool's Day in 1977 when Bob and I first met even as I write this story over thirty years later.

One Year Later, April 22, We Married . . .

Our marriage vows included the well-known line, ". . . for better, for worse, for richer, for poorer, in sickness and in health, until death do us part." We married, in 1978, in the church where I had grown up. It became clear to me over the years why this line is included in marriage vows. We certainly had the poorer part of our marriage and are still waiting on the "richer" part. We also definitely have had the better and worse, sickness and health parts of our vows. Not just the flu-type of sickness, but also emotional, spiritual, and chronic-illness types of sicknesses. Plus, I went deaf. There were, and still are, however, more "better" times in our lives together than "worse."

We actually joke at times about our physical limitations. I didn't believe Bob when he told me that he was blind in one eye when we met. It wasn't until I asked his mother about it that the fact of this sank in for me. She said that Bob had been blind in one eye since he was twelve. When he was five, he contracted a high fever and it damaged the retina of his left eye to the point that it gradually flaked away over time. He could only see shadows when we met in 1977. They could repair the eye in the early stages of such a fever today, but not back in the 1950s when it happened to Bob. I still remember the day he said, "It's [the vision] completely gone." Of course, I was hard of hearing when we met and later became deaf. We like to tell people,

My husband Bob and myself.

"Well, we were attracted to each other because Bob could only see half of me and I could only hear half of what he said."

As it turned out, though, Bob has said many good things that I missed until my cochlear implant was activated in May of 2002. Now, Bob says, "I can't get away with anything anymore!"

Our long-time friends, Don and Barbara Heckman of Virginia, taught us how to dance. They were competitive ballroom dancers and teachers. At their encouragement, we drove to Gahanna once a week for several months to learn round dancing, which is ballroom dancing to cues, much like square dancing with callers. We both loved the lessons, and since I could still hear music at the time, I relished this atmosphere. I memorized the unique cues for each song.

One night, after we had learned many dances, the teacher said he was going to call different cues to make sure we were listening—but Liz, here, did not hear *that* cue. I loved the song and off we went dancing in our unified circle with all the other couples.

I knew what cues normally came with this song and started doing the step in which the couples dance circling away from their partners and returning to each other and dance forward together. When I came back around, it was another couple and Bob was way ahead—dancing alone. I scooted to his side and he explained what happened later.

That was our last dance lesson.

I wrote this poem January 12, 1997, at a time when I was feeling he was getting the raw end of the deal in our "for better or for worse" vows. Often I have said that since Bob had to learn some sign language and do face-to-face or TTY communication with me, it was like learning French or living in a new country.

You Didn't Know

January 12, 1997

You didn't know when you married me
That you would have to move to France;
Learn a new language and learn how to dance.
You didn't know twenty years ago
That "for better or for worse" would be something you would
    know.

We really don't have to move to France
And we both really wanted to learn how to dance.
But a new language we now are learning
And I know, in your heart, it is not your yearning.

To say life is full of "signs" is true
And since the day I married you
We have had many signs to show us the way:
Neither of us knew that signs would be here to stay.

You are so handy with a hammer and drill
But this is one thing that you just can't fix
So instead every day we are improving our skills
To be able to talk and continue to fill

Our lives together with love and laughter
To know that the silence won't last forever,
But our love will last
And that is what matters.

Not only did Bob learn enough sign to help with our communication, he bought me a TTY in December 1996 and one for our daughter, Mary. She had married and was living in California while we were living in Ohio. This latter purchase was a complete surprise. The night after I had my TTY, the phone rang, and as had become our custom, Bob answered. He told me I had a TTY call. I was bewildered because I had not met anyone [in one day] who had a TTY nor knew of anyone who would call me. Bob saw my expression and smiled his kind of funny smile as I raced to answer via my TTY.

I typed, "Hi, this is Liz, GA." GA stands for Go Ahead. The message that came back was, "Hi Mom!" I was puzzled and then reasoned that Mary had rented a TTY or something. I hesitated and she came back saying, "Surprise! Dad thought you would be surprised. I have been so excited all day waiting for my new TTY to arrive and to call you. Dad bought it for me for Christmas."

I was overwhelmed and honestly don't remember what I said, but I had to be exclaiming how excited I was. By then, Bob was looking over my shoulder and smiling that wonderful grin of his. So Mary and I talked and talked. It was heaven on earth. Since she had married, I had not really been able to talk to her on the phone. We had always talked about important things over the years and now she was having her first child. So the next month or so our phone bills were high but no one really cared because we all knew we had a lot of catching up to do.

How do you thank someone who is that sensitive and caring? I didn't have the answer but I wrote him a poem. Marriage is work even when you have perfect health, money, and no rough spots in your lives. But it is work that is well worth the end result; I'll take it and keep it close.

My daughter Mary and her husband Bob.

We had a blended family before it was common and no books had been written as guides. We were both left with debts from our prior marriages and began our marriage with no savings, but plenty of love. Bob went completely blind in one eye and I went deaf. In the middle of all this, I was diagnosed with multiple sclerosis. In 1987, there was maybe one book about MS on the market and no drug therapy developed yet. We moved fifteen times, including a move from Ohio to Seattle and back, in one year, a move from Ohio to Phoenix and back, in one year also, another move to Phoenix and next we landed in the Seattle area again. We missed our Ohio roots and, in 2005, we made what we hope is our final move back home when we landed in Grove City, where, ironically I began my first beat as a reporter.

But even with partial blindness, deafness, blended family concerns, MS, fifteen moves, job and career changes, at this writing Bob and I are moving into our thirtieth year of marriage feeling strong in each other's arms. We renewed our vows on our twenty-fifth anniversary.

Bob and I had moved to Arizona, again—our second desert adventure—and our dear friend Don Huiner and his sister Jan and brother-in-law Tom were planning a visit to our new "casa." Don and his late wife and our close friend, Eileen, had a renewal of vows ceremony on their 25th anniversary and I thought it would work for us, too. Knowing Don, Jan and Tom were coming, we planned a simple ceremony at the Baptist church we were attending in Glendale, Arizona. We had met with the pastor and picked our music and scripture, leaving the rest to the pastor.

At the last minute, we asked Don and Jan to stand up with us and they agreed. Tom would take photos. We invited ten friends we knew from work and from our last journey in the desert. We had a gathering at our home first, serving a simple meal and having some time to visit. Don, Jan, and Tom swore they weren't tired, even though they had arrived that same afternoon.

Bob and I dressed for the occasion and we all headed to the church. I was carrying pink miniature lilies and baby's breath I had purchased at the Safeway florist shop that same day. The ceremony began and we walked smiling down the aisle. Our friends were in the front pew of the church.

The pastor performed a loving service and I had selected the music. I neglected to check the length of time on the songs and some were four minutes long. Bob and I held hands, facing each other smiling and talking quietly. My feet hurt from shoes I'd not worn for ages. I asked the pastor to stop the music but he just smiled. It got funny waiting for the songs to end. Jan whispered that she needed to sit down because the time change and the fatigue of the trip had finally hit her.

We chuckled and thanked the pastor and our friends and went home married—again.

As we both age, together, we hold each other up mentally, physically and spiritually and that makes our marriage work. Oh yes, I must mention forgiveness because without that in our lives, we would be very alone.

File It Away

Having been a secretary for more than 25 years, one thing I never enjoyed was filing. It's important for you to know this little fact to understand the following poem I wrote in January 1997. Coping with hearing loss is not easy. It is a mourning process similar to losing a loved one. I treasured sounds—music, laughter, conversation, nature sounds—just about everything. Losing that ability was painful and to say differently would be a lie.

Remember, though, as you read this poem, that in 2002 all this changed. In 1997, I had no clue this loss would be regained by a cochlear implant. This poem speaks to my letting go of some of the pain and moving on.

File It Away

How long ago has it been?
I can barely remember when
We could talk in the dark
Quiet and soft
And have no problem listening.

How long ago has it been?
Since I listened without struggling?
Or you spoke from the heart
Without having to start
Over and over again?

How long ago has it been?
Too many years in between
And the memory fades
Of an easy day,
Of hearing without any strain.
So, how long ago has it been?
I cannot remember when,
So I'll let the thought fade
And let it rest in the shade.
It's history, so I'll file it away.

As I wrote this poem, I was surprised as the words hit the page. I
realized I had been mouthing the words, prior to this time saying,
"It's OK, I'm OK, Don't worry about me, I'm handling it fine." But
I was reaching a healthy state of mind here and now I was getting excited about the possibilities of my future.

Flashing Lights and Jumping Dogs

Ever since I worked at Battelle Memorial Institute (BMI) in Columbus, Ohio, I have been a self-made technology nut. I began working
at BMI in 1978. The nearly ten years I spent working as a secretary at
BMI, I was always in the computer department. After Mike Tikson,
department manager at the time, hired me as his secretary, my life
began to change.

The computer mainframe on the sixth floor was huge. Desktops
were a dream of the future. As Mike progressed up the ladder of
management, he took me along. By the time I was an Executive Secretary, he had a desktop computer on his credenza, yet all 600 plus

secretaries were still using IBM Correcting Selectrics typewriters. But this made perfect sense as they were testing the technology around 1981. I remember watching a woman named Sue testing the first mouse being developed. I was dumbfounded as to how it might ever work. I remember saying, "Sue, that will never catch on. How odd," but she just smiled. Good thing my name isn't Bill Gates.

Mike often traveled to our other installations in the United States and Europe. During one of his longer trips, I did two things. One was good, the other not.

He was an avid reader and issues of the *Wall Street Journal* and various technology magazines and papers were stacked throughout his office. I cleaned it thoroughly. My reasoning was that he was a retired U.S. Air Force colonel and I thought the neatness would please him.

Now, you fellow secretaries are thinking, "Oh no, Liz, you never do that." You are correct.

The other task I took upon myself was to put his calendar on his desktop computer. It was an early form of Outlook Express. This was a good thing.

Upon Mike's return, he walked into his office and seeing that it was neat and organized, he sighed. "Liz, what have you done? I won't be able to find a thing!" I apologized and felt terrible. Since then I have learned that a cluttered desk is a sign of intelligence and there is no doubt in my mind that he was highly intelligent. Needless to say, I never did that again.

Now that he had seen the desk, though, I was holding my breath because I had to let him know about his computer and what I had done. After some time passed, I told him about the calendar and showed him the areas I had worked in. I let him know that it was fun for me and that I would delete it all, if he so chose.

Instead, in his fashion, he picked up the phone and made a call. I motioned, "Do you want me to leave?" and he said to stay. Then I heard him say, "This is Mike Tikson. Come down to my office and put this desktop computer on Liz's desk."

As far as I knew, I was the first secretary to have a desktop computer at BMI. I used inter-departmental e-mail and played with the technology. Not long after that, Xerox marketed Memorywriters into which you inserted a 5½-inch floppy disk and saved your typing to that disk. When Steve, the typewriter shop technician, brought it to me and explained how to use it, I kept asking, "But *how* does it work?"

He gave me the best piece of advice and one I continue to use today, "Don't worry about *how* it works and just *make* it work." And I did and thrived.

Mike told me more than once that computers were the wave of the future for secretaries and to learn as much as I could about them. I did. It wasn't long after this that many secretaries had desktop computers and the world of office life changed. Little did I know, at that time, that computers and all technology were going to play a major role in my quality of life. This time was a training ground for me and by the time I was almost deaf, technology had jumped leaps and bounds into the future.

Technology Has Made Huge Difference for Hard of Hearing
May 20, 1998

The letters HOPE could easily stand for Hang On People and Enjoy. Enjoy life. You may wonder, as many do, how I enjoy life so much because I usually don't hear the birds singing, understand words when someone is singing a song and often cannot grasp the conversation of more than one person at a time (and in a controlled, quiet atmosphere).

Closed captioning is a must for television and movie viewing, a light awakens me along with my hearing dog, a TTY (text telephone), and the (Ohio) Relay Service and e-mail are my links to other people. Basically, my life was turned upside down when my hearing loss became profound. How so? you might ask. What do I mean by upside down? Now I look at life differently, from a new perspective. You see,

I had many years to enjoy music, hear birds sing, understand conversations, talk on the phone and awaken with the same annoying buzz you might jump to each morning.

There are many benefits to my life, as a hard of hearing person. I have been given an opportunity to look at life with a fresh view. The past is part of who I am today, so I utilize my experiences, draw on my strengths, focus on what I can do and decided not to waste energy worrying about what I might be missing. In the process, I want to help others understand more clearly what hard of hearing people, and their families, experience on a daily basis. I believe we all have the ability to be over comers, no matter the circumstance, and look at life with a spirit of hope and anticipation.

I mentioned closed captioning as a necessity for me, but before 1993 no television had this capability and a special box was required. Now it is mandatory; all televisions 13″ or larger must have this capability. My TTY is small and can be used as a regular phone as well (a bonus for my hearing family). The first TTY was very large, not at all portable and cumbersome to use. Wakening to a light is another bonus, but I think about what people who were Deaf or hard of hearing did before this technology.

How did these people waken for work if the entire household was Deaf or hard of hearing or they lived alone? How did they communicate before TTY's, e-mail and the Relay Service? Imagine making an emergency phone call. No wonder people felt isolated.

In my lifetime, all this technology became reality. That is something to celebrate and enjoy. Losing our hearing does not mean you automatically become a grump and a drudge. So I hang on and enjoy because the alternative is lonely and a waste of life.

Since this writing, I have seen documentaries about the ingenious ways people who were Deaf woke themselves and how they relied on hearing friends and family for communication prior to technology advances. No doubt technology has smoothed out many aspects of our lives with hearing loss or deafness, keeping us connected. But what makes us feel linked is another living being. Friends, family and even occasional strangers make our lives more meaningful.

One particular member of my family makes my life warmer and gentler. In 1995, Bob and I were living in Arizona. We were "empty nesters" and rather enjoying our life together for the first time as two adults. When we married, I had Mary, four, and Bob had Mike, six, and Lisa, eight. We missed our grown children but enjoyed this phase of our marriage. We also missed our pets that had either died or been given to other homes, for various reasons.

We wanted another longhaired dachshund like our former pet, Molly. She was a cuddler. We watched newspaper ads and found a family with seven dachshund pups, one longhaired. The parents of the pups were there, too, and we gravitated right to the longhaired pup. The family was happy we chose him, but also sad. It seems he was their favorite so they lined up with this pup they had named Midnight and took pictures. I had never seen anything quite like it. We assured them he would be loved and cared for. We never had the heart to tell them that the name we gave to Midnight was Snert.

Our puppy learned fast and certainly loved to cuddle. He was only three pounds and could not step over a garden hose on the grass. He learned to come to me when I said, in caretaker speech (like we talk to babies), "How'd you get so pretty, Snert?" and he would run and jump into my lap. I trained him to trust me by my sitting on one chair and stretching my legs to another, making a bridge. Bob would put him on the other chair and I talked to Snert until he learned to walk across my legs and into my arms. Then he was praised as his tail wagged incessantly.

We moved back to Ohio in 1996. I was searching for work but my hearing loss prevented any "high level" secretarial work and I began again at entry level. This same year, I learned about Lions Hearing Dogs and the training they offered for pets to become certified hearing dogs. I inquired with the trainer, Cathy Nagaich, and began the process. When she learned that Snert was a cute breed, she was unsure if he would work. "He may be too cute," she told me. We proceeded

Snert and me.

through the pre-testing and I took him to her vet for examination. Cathy brought her two school-aged children with her.

While Snert was up on the cold, steel table and the vet was poking his hind end, Snert was licking the faces of Cathy's children and wagging his tail. Cathy saw this and said, "OK. That's enough. He is perfect."

Hearing dogs must be very tolerant and friendly—never nippy. If ever a dog was going to nip, it would have been then.

Snert and I worked together at home on his obedience training—"Stay," "Sit," "Come," and so forth. Cathy gave up on "lie down" because we could never tell if he was sitting or lying down because he is so close to the floor or ground.

He finished his training in six months, not the typical year. He passed his test as if he knew he was being tested, almost showing off, but I loved him for it. He has proved many times to be an asset in my life and a good friend.

Helper Dogs Present Unique Chance to Show Our Patience

December 9, 1998

It is only one to four hours of your life. You may be flying to Chicago or as far as Texas or California. It is still only a few hours of your life. You can read, sleep, work on your laptop computer, write letters, eat—whatever your preference. All are on their way to or from somewhere and anxious to arrive.

Now add a twist. You are traveling with your helper dog. Your dog may be a large Labrador retriever or a small dachshund. You go to your seat and a fellow traveler refuses to move to let you take your seat. Or whines he does not sit next to dogs. You pray for a flight attendant to handle the situation. Usually it works out, but it makes the flight very uncomfortable.

Recently a friend of mine, who happens to be legally blind and hard of hearing, was flying from Arizona to Columbus, Ohio. She had upgraded to first class. She and her guide dog, a beautiful, white lab, went to sit and the man in the aisle seat refused to move. The flight attendant handled it poorly. She also ignored the ADA laws requiring assistance to people with helper dogs. She asked if anyone would move to allow her to sit. Not one person responded. The man smiled in strange victory as my friend and her dog were sent to the back of the plane.

Does this scenario strike a nerve and cause anger or disbelief? How can we handle such insensitivity? This country has lived through similar scenarios with much pain involved.

I was met with a similar situation with a much different outcome. My hearing dog weighs only 15 pounds—he is a longhaired dachshund. Again a man refused to move out of my window seat. He said, "I don't sit next to dogs." But the flight attendant was a champion. She simply told him to move to his seat and if he didn't like the dog he could move to the back of the plane. She then proceeded to bring Snert, my hearing dog, a bowl of ice chips. Later she brought a blanket and a pillow. We chuckled. She was anxious to know all about Snert as my hearing dog. The man seemed to cower a little.

Most people I meet while traveling are patient and interested in learning about hearing dogs. Traveling is then a pleasure for all involved. My speech is good so many don't grasp why I need a hearing

Snert became a hearing dog.

dog. They cannot see my hearing loss. So I educate. Most helper dogs are thought to be physically assistive dogs, thus, large and not small and cuddly like my Snert.

"What does he do for you?" is the most common question—and a good one. I explain that he was trained through Lions Hearing Dogs in my own home. I selected three sounds to have him trained to alert me. I chose smoke detector, doorbell-door knocking and alarm clock. He never lets me oversleep.

He naturally warns me of anything out of place, even squirrels and rabbits running through his yard. He senses danger in some individuals and I exit those situations. Quoting his vet: "Dogs have 40,000 times the instincts of humans. Trust his instincts." My dog is a joy, so naturally he travels with me.

Helper dogs are loving companions. They make our lives easier, more complete and independent. To be refused by a stranger, especially for the short term, is baffling, frustrating and leaves a feeling of sadness that is difficult to explain. I ask each of you to please be patient when you see someone with a helper dog. If you love animals and the thought of displaying the aforementioned behavior abhors you, then I applaud you. I thank you for the many who require this assistance.

If you don't like animals, or fear them, I ask for an extra amount of patience—for just a few hours of your life. These helper dogs may change your mind about animals. You may be uncomfortable for a short time. How do you think my friend felt standing in the aisle of a plane with her dog and all the first class passengers refusing to move or assist her? And the flight attendant displaying preference to those who need no obvious assistance? And, I must state again, ignoring her legal and humane obligations to help my friend?

How about we all attempt to get on the plane called *understanding*? Or *acceptance*? We are all on our personal journeys. We all have our struggles and triumphs. Sorrows and joys. Our destinations are all different. The next time a furry, four-legged helper dog enters your life, even for a short time, look into the eyes of the owner. Look into the eyes of the helper dog.

Then look into your own heart. With whatever it takes, muster up enough compassion to comply for this short time. You might even smile in triumph. Not that you "won" but that you stretched your limits. I believe it could also make you more open to receive gentleness and kindness in your own life.

And the furry creature will quietly walk out of your life with a wag in its tail, the owner with a smile on his or her face and a positive story to share. It will be a win-win situation for all.

By now it must be obvious that my hearing dog is special to me. He is so cute and loves people. When someone comes to the door, he is right there barking and then rolling over to greet them. People say he is cute and I respond, "And he knows it."

I wrote the following poem in 1997 about Snert. I was still able to walk him and we strolled every morning before I went to work and often in the early evening. Weekends we were out often so we knew all our neighbors. I performed at Deaf Poetry in the Park the same year and Bob brought him up on stage for me. He was a hit (Snert *and* Bob).

"The Best Way to Meet Your Neighbors"

The best way to meet your neighbors
Is to have a cute and friendly dog.
Walk him up and down the street
And they'll come out to meet the dog.

Snert is our dog's name, his claim to fame
And he loves all the people he meets.
He will lick your toes, if they're exposed
And hopes you will give him a treat.

He does not care if you have no hair
Or if your clothes might be a little square
He will kiss your face if you don't turn away,
And remember your house, and always stop there to play.

He has so much to give and just hopes to live
With a wag in his tail and a gentle heartbeat.
And wants to know everyone who lives on his street
And also their dogs so he can play with them, too.

So no matter your age, Snert just wants to play
He just wants to be your best friend.
We can learn from him and the lesson is this:
Meet all your neighbors and give all our lives a lift.
(But Snert will give you a kiss.)

Listening and Hearing

I talk to my dog, Snert, and our Golden Retriever, Jack, all the time. I know they listen—but when they are in the hot pursuit of a rabbit, they only hear me but don't heed what I say. They seem to like the sound of our voices and are comforted when we talk to them. It is therapeutic for Bob and me. More than once, we will hear the other talking and say, "What did you say?" and we respond that we were talking to Jack or Snert—then we laugh.

When it comes to humans interacting, it is much more complex and takes energy we may not always possess at any given moment. During the process of losing my hearing, I continued to talk easily. It is natural for me. Listening had to be learned and I believe my lack of ability to hear helped me sharpen my listening skills. Active listening is the common name for what I did and still do. I use all my senses to listen.

Good Listening Is Not a Passive Activity

May 12, 1999

How many people would admit they talk to their dog? I do. I ask him questions such as, "Do you have to go out?" or "Are you hungry?" Why do I do this? He tilts his head back and forth giving the appearance he is listening and understanding. Even though he never answers, I persist. He understands some English. I have heard that dogs can potentially understand up to 100 words: "There's a squirrel in the yard," and "Want to go for a walk?"

He is smart but a champion bluffer most of the time. He listens intently but most of his reaction depends on the inflection of my voice or whether I am holding his leash. Dogs may read a true form of body language. We all read body language, to some degree. Courses in assertiveness show how different stances convey various messages.

Sometimes when people are talking with me, they will stop and ask if I can hear them. I better watch that I'm not tilting my head back and forth, like my dog. I appreciate their concern and their desire to communicate effectively. Usually I really am listening. Intently. And thinking.

With age, the thought process slows, but it is more refined. Listening is an art: really listening and caring about what is being spoken, especially when you may not agree with what you are hearing. I have found this to be a genuine benefit of living with hearing loss. Because I want to hear, I seriously work at listening. I believe this to be true of the majority of people who have some degree of hearing loss.

Remember the Simon and Garfunkel song, "The Sound of Silence"? One line I love is "People hearing without listening." I try not to do this. Well, actually I can't. Instead, I utilize every option available to me: reading body language and facial expressions, listening to voice inflection and actual voice, sizing up the situation, repeating what I hear for clarity, positioning myself to see best, hearing aids, the written word, sign language (when appropriate, and sign includes much body language), informing people up front that I am hard of hearing, and often using an FM Listening System.

Well, you name it and I have probably used that method to improve communication. Why? The main reason is to let others know I really care about what they are saying. I truly do. Also, I am a very social person; I love people. I don't want to be cut off. A small part of me wants to prove to myself, and others, that I can continue to communicate, even as my hearing worsens. Yes, it calls for more effort for everyone involved, but I am hoping the end result is worth it. I feel it is.

My Grandmother Page used to tell me, "Patience is a virtue, Elizabeth." It took years for me to understand what she meant. Life experience brought me closer to understanding. Anyone who struggles with a diminished ability to function in a way the world deems "normal," has learned about patience with oneself first, then others.

Life can be difficult enough, patience wears thin at times, and we feel anything but virtuous. I can only suggest that we get up each day, strive to do our best, and believe that each person is doing the same. No matter the situation, or our ability to hear, we can still endeavor to care: to put on our "best ears" and really listen, not just hear. I want to believe that my dog is trying to know what I am saying to him. In the same light, I want everyone I meet to believe that I really try to know what they are saying.

I know it is tiring, at times, but it's a fact that I cannot change about myself. It is part of who I am and I have come to accept that. The millions with hearing loss are often walking around in a cloud of silence. We may feel outside of the everyday world. From that cloud we can choose to stay separate or become a part. Even when my dog doesn't really know what I am saying, he still accepts me. I accept him with his "limitations."

There is beauty in everything created. When we dwell on this thought, even a bare tree in winter holds promise. What might appear to have little reason for existence most likely is filled with purpose. We may need to water and nurture the tree so that it will come to full growth. People want to be appreciated and encouraged. Then the full purpose of each life will come to fruition.

If we really listen, we may be amazed at what we hear, what we learn. A little encouragement goes a long, long way. I believe if your heart is in the right place, it will come back to you in full measure.

Enjoy the Ride

If you have ever been to San Francisco, you will understand this column completely. Driving in San Francisco is a real adventure. To use the streets of San Francisco in an analogy, I could say—no matter how corny it sounds—that the streets in this hilly city are similar to the ups and downs in life. Whether you are the driver or the passenger, life is a series of climbs and dives.

Visualize San Francisco in the early 1970s, a stick-shift Chevy Vega, and a young, novice driver and you should be able to see me popping around downtown San Francisco.

I'm Still Grinding Gears on Life's Hills

April 12, 2000

As I started my car, I found myself laughing loudly at myself. The noise that emitted from my car must have sounded horrible. The car was already started, yet I could not hear the engine and so I tried to turn the key. You know the noise.

As I laughed I thought, "When will you learn to watch for the lights, Elizabeth?" Was this conversation with myself telling me to adapt to my deafness? No, because I was laughing and not feeling stupid or ridiculous, but rather funny. I have adapted, but occasionally situations are hilarious.

Adjusting to gradual hearing loss, to me, is similar to learning to shift gears. At first, you avoid inclines because you know you will roll backward until you press on the clutch and get it in the right gear. The inclines I avoided regarding hearing loss were situations when there was no one nearby to hear for me.

I realize now I should have honed in on better communication skills earlier in life, learned to advocate earlier. However one should not live on regrets but learn from them. "Wise men learn by other men's mistakes, fools by their own," H.G. Bohn stated. I think we learn from both. But there is much less egg on our face when we learn from others' mistakes. I hope I am helping readers keep egg off their face.

I remember driving in downtown San Francisco in the early 1970s—not recommended—in my old car in which I learned to shift gears. I was still a novice. I prayed for all green lights, but eventually I had to stop at a red light on a huge hill. When the light turned green, I opened my door and motioned to the driver behind me to please back up. I remember the driver laughed, but he did back up. Maybe this action is common in cities like San Francisco, but it was very new to me. I remember feeling embarrassed. As my face burned with shame, I puttered to the top of the hill and sought out flatlands immediately.

I wonder if that type of action is adapting or asking someone else to simply make things easier. I could have practiced shifting gears on hills more often instead of avoiding them. Whether this stubborn attitude was simply a sign of youth or a lack of foresight, I may never figure out, but I do drive an automatic car now.

It is 26 years since this incident and I have learned, through life's ups and downs, how to talk and write about my hearing loss, how to laugh at the funny situations and not take myself too seriously. That's why I laughed after making that grinding noise in my car.

Children laugh hundreds of times a day, yet adults often forget this healthy exercise. Just watch children playing, with their heads often tossing back in sheer delight and maybe all they did was miss a step while jumping rope. "Laugh and the world laughs with you, Weep and you weep alone," the opening lines of the 1883 poem "Solitude" by Ella Wheeler Wilcox, are wise words.

Life with progressive hearing loss is not an easy road to follow. Being a survivor of the '6os, I remember that the word "advocate" meant someone who held his or her fist up high and tight while fighting for a cause. Time has taught me, along with Webster's dictionary that this word does mean "one who supports or defends a cause." But the fist-holding part I decided to eliminate from my advocacy efforts. For I was not—and am not—angry. I was basically uninformed and apathetic. Hiding from reality does not make it easier to cope. The reality of my progressive deafness has become very real to me. So I practice shifting gears as I ride through life.

I remind myself to watch for the lights on the control panel of my car. Yes, I drive an automatic car, but in life we still must learn to shift gears or how to adjust to change. Change is a certainty and present throughout our lives. We should all practice on hillsides to learn how to shift into gear and keep going upward. We may stall occasionally and have to restart our lives. We can determine to restart with new energy, finding what energizes us.

Going downhill takes thought, too. We know another hill is in the future, so we may choose to coast for awhile or rest and recuperate, preparing for the next change. Shifting gears is a challenge, but a challenge we can learn to meet with courage. I still don't think I would want to drive the streets of San Francisco today, but I know I could. I simply choose not to. Besides, the streetcars are a lot more fun and I could get in some good, healthy laughter, making some good memories in the process. Enjoy the ride, for life is so short.

Employee/Employer Blues

From my first typical, college-bound job waitressing at eighteen, then selling shoes, being a receiving clerk, working my way to executive secretary, later as a reporter, and finally as a teacher's aide at fifty-two, lessons were learned that, at the time, seemed pointless, especially in the early years. But income was necessary to pay for books, then rent, groceries, medical bills; well, you know the drill, the list can be endless. I was learning integrity in the work place, although it would be years before I could give these lessons a name.

People I have talked with have similar horror stories of jobs they carried out to survive and build a resume. My horror stories include working in a furniture refinishing shop where the first thing I did in the morning was kill the bugs that had come up *through* my desk while the workers were in the back smoking something that smelled really odd. That was in 1971 in California. This same business was shut down for back taxes. On that day, I was filing and two men in overcoats and slouch hats (really, just like the movies of old) came in and asked my name while they ran a wire and lock through the handles of the filing cabinet. Probably another reason filing is not a favorite activity of mine.

One man said, "Get your final pay in cash now and leave. Don't come back or talk with anyone." So I went to my boss and said I needed my final pay in cash and he handed me a 100-dollar bill and said, "That should cover it." I was making minimum wage which was about two dollars an hour. I think that covered it.

We all have our war stories of jobs where we're fired with no explanation, or where we have experienced trouble in the work place because we could not hear "well enough" to suit our employer, no accommodations were offered, and we didn't know how to ask. Many of us didn't know our rights, and until 1990, when the Americans with Disabilities Act (ADA) was signed, we might not have had any.

Before the ADA, people using wheelchairs had no way to get on a city bus. People needing an interpreter because of deafness could not expect the request to be filled by employers. Getting a TTY or FM Listening System was like pulling teeth with many employers, even with our best manners and negotiating skills. Employers generally did not want the extra expense or liability added to their budget. Even today this holds true for many businesses.

Both sides had legitimate arguments and there are many excellent employers willing to work with their staff, if they know what their needs are. I am not bashing employers but stating the fact that people with disabilities simply must work harder. And their employers must also work harder—thus conflicts can arise.

Over my work years, I have been fortunate in having someone in each work place who was willing to go the extra mile and work with me. This really became an issue from 1996 to 1999. I was working in the medical field with nurses and physicians in a peer review organization. I loved the work, even though I had to begin at entry level. It was a fact that I was going to have to prove my value in the work place, even though I had some 20 years of experience. This may not seem fair, but life is not always fair.

Here I had to ask for the FM Listening System and a TTY to be able to take part in constant meetings and to be able to talk with clients efficiently. I requested Anna from Columbus Speech and Hearing Center in Columbus, Ohio to come and give a demo on these systems to staff who would be doing the purchasing. Anna did great and sold them on the idea of both assistive devices and, in about one week, they were in my cubicle ready to set up. I thanked them more than once and proceeded to use these devices to improve my ability to do my job well and become a more vital part of internal teams.

Hard of Hearing Employees Need Your Patience

February 10, 1999

Twenty-seven years of secretarial experience has been challenging. It is a very rewarding profession and one I am proud to be a part of. The challenges, in many ways, have been unique for me. I started out never wanting to do secretarial work until I met my first electric typewriter. Then it was memory writers and then computers, e-mail, and fax machines. I am from the old school of cut and paste and carbon paper. So all the office advancements are truly a blessing.

My ability to hear has declined slowly since childhood. I managed fine for many years. Or did I? I must confess, I bluffed often and relied on lip reading even before I realized I was doing those things. My hearing loss has become profound in the last five to seven years.

For some time, I was in a quandary about what to do about my work situation. I considered returning to school and starting a new profession where hearing was not a requirement. I was still very efficient at my work but my self-esteem and self-confidence were falling flat. Taking minutes and notes, in my own shorthand, was a part of my work for years. During the last few months, even though I utilize an FM listening system in meetings, I have had to accept the fact that I can no longer effectively take minutes.

Lip reading a group, sometimes talking at the same time, is virtually impossible. It was another step in the acceptance process. My thinking was that I needed to continue to struggle through to "keep my job" or hold on to the familiar. But my work place is a healthy one. When I discussed this openly with my supervisors, it was easily accepted. "There are others who can do that for you," I was told. What a pleasant response. I offered to carry some of their workload to balance them doing some of my work. So far, so good.

The acceptance process I speak of has been long and arduous. Since my hearing has declined slowly, my acceptance of this loss had a similar speed. To learn how to still function effectively without the use of one of my integral senses was awesome. Challenging. Rewarding. Often frightening. Frightening, you ask? Yes.

Would I be able to continue to work as a secretary? I can't use the regular phone. I can't take minutes. I struggle to understand conversations with more than one person speaking—but I have learned that hearing people have this same struggle—and I rely on mechanical devices to hear anything.

Learning to advocate for oneself is interesting. First, I had to determine my needs and how to satisfy those needs to function to the best of my ability. Some options you might want to explore if you have a hearing loss: better hearing aids, FM listening systems, amplified phones, flashing alarms, TTY-text telephone, sign language classes, lip-speech reading training, and a hearing dog.

Second, I researched how to best utilize the enhancements in my daily routine. Third, I determined my level of responsibility in supplying these improvements to my quality of life. Often, I needed to approach my employer to assist in the work place.

I then proceeded to negotiate with the appropriate people. I prepared all the information to present my ideas clearly and schedule a hands-on demo, if necessary. I allowed time for this part of the process to happen. An open, communicative and patient approach served me well. An appreciative response, when my requests were granted, was essential.

Communication is the key. We all desire to function to the best of our ability. We hard of hearing folks have some unique challenges and needs to function at our optimum level. My hope is that more employers respond with the same open-mindedness as mine.

I utilize a TTY at work and make all my calls through the Ohio Relay Service. At first, I was nervous calling customers, wondering if they would balk at using this form of communication. Absolutely everyone uses it well and few seem to mind the extra effort. It is possible they are merely tolerating, but that is to be expected with something so unique. Using this form of communication can be very interesting. One person speaks at a time and the other party cannot speak until the other says, "go ahead."

I continue on as a secretary, better identified in this age as assistant. I love what I do and through time have learned ways to persevere. It has been worth it. I have learned much about my abilities and acceptance of my limitations. I know we all have some degree of limitation, some struggle we call our own. There can be a true sense of camaraderie when we realize this fact. Each day I take a deep breath and dig in to the best of my ability.

We all know it takes just one person to mess up a good thing. Within the next year after this column appeared, I had a new boss who had no patience with my deafness or my worsening MS. Even though she was a nurse, her compassion level was low. I saw the writing on the wall and sought other work. The very day she scheduled a meeting to let me go, I walked in and handed her my letter of resignation. I have to admit, it felt good to have the upper hand, but she would have had a huge fight on her hands had she tried to prove I was not doing my job.

Most of my work life was good. From 1978 to 1987, I was fortunate to work at Battelle Memorial Institute in Columbus, Ohio. I began at entry level with my secretarial work and soon moved to more responsibility. The man who gave me a chance, even when others said he should not, was Michael Tikson. He managed the computer department and was a retired U.S. Air Force colonel.

He was quite tall with white, wavy hair and a ready smile. When I interviewed to work for him, my competition was stiff. Many women had much more experience than I. His secretary, Barbara Weed, was retiring and was hoping I would fill her spot.

One day, Mr. Tikson (which I *always* called him out of respect) came to my office door and said, "Liz, will you come with me?" Of course I did. We walked down the long hallway on the 10th floor of Building 11 and he said he wanted to offer me the job of department secretary. He was talking and my mouth was stuck open. I was amazed he had chosen me. A twenty-five-year-old, fairly naïve woman.

When we sat in his office, he smiled and said, "You do want the job, don't you?" I realized I had not said a word. My secretarial experience was unremarkable. I told him, "Yes!"

He said other managers had advised him not to hire me, due to my inexperience, but I would learn Mr. Tikson had his own mind. He apparently saw something in me others had not; he believed in me and said so.

I worked diligently for him from 1979 until we moved to Seattle in 1987. He received promotions and took me with him, making my last job title that of executive secretary. My hearing was waning slowly but he and I never had any difficulty.

Shortly after I left, he retired from Battelle. Evan Brill, another manager whom I had worked with, contacted me in Seattle to let me know he was throwing a party for him and asked if I could make it. Over the course of his career Mr. Tikson had only four secretaries, and Evan was trying to get us all there.

I had been diagnosed with MS and I knew many people in Ohio were concerned about me. So Bob and I flew back for the party, surprising everyone but Evan. It was a great party and after we visited family, we headed home to Seattle.

One year, after we had moved back to Ohio, shortly before "Secretaries' Day," Mike called and said he wanted to take me out to lunch. I was doing database work then and very little secretarial work, and my poor hearing was a big issue (a negative one) at my current job. But he and I had a great lunch and caught up on how our grown children were doing.

When our daughter, Mary, was married in 1995, the Tiksons came and celebrated with us. He was sporting a gray beard and looked statelier than ever. This would be the last time I would see him until 1999.

The following column is very special to me and I hope to never forget this day. God gave me the ability to hear well enough this day to hear a dying man's loving words.

I'm Getting Better at Saying Good-Bye

August 8, 1999

Saying good-bye has always been difficult for me. Recently I went to say good-bye to a dear friend of more than 20 years. He was a mentor, teacher, inspiration, but most of all a true friend, accepting of everyone. When I went to his home, I did not know what to expect about his illness. I had not asked prior to the visit, assuming his heart had weakened more: only physically, not spiritually. When I saw him bed ridden, and I looked into his eyes I saw him there.

We held hands and talked, talked about what matters in this life, nothing trivial. We each had things to say to one another that could not be left unsaid. I don't think I blinked more than once. He was weak and I concentrated on his every word, on every gentle squeeze he made with his hand, his inner turmoil in working to communicate so I could understand. It was not easy for either of us, but so necessary. For the next 24 hours, it was all I could think about, I dreamt about our visit and awoke with it on my mind. I didn't find that troublesome because it was a profound experience that I never want to forget.

My emotions are a mixture of loss, sadness, and extreme fulfillment. Loss of someone important for almost half of my life thus far, sadness that he was so ill, but fulfillment that I followed God's insistence that I overcome any of my personal fears and meet certain death in the face. My friend told me that he was not afraid to die. That he was ready. Even in his impending death, this giving man was still teaching me. He was showing me how to die without fear. How to leave this life on earth with grace and honor. I know God met him and said, "Well done, my good and faithful servant."

How unselfish he was with the little time we spent together. His words were meant to comfort me and if I turned the conversation toward him, he would smile weakly and say "But . . ." and turn it back to me. We both needed this time to say good-bye.

The hospice was praised by the family. They were working with his young grandchildren to create a memory book of Papa. Counseling and medical explanations were readily available. This is not the first time I have heard such praise of similar hospices. My friend's wife and I talked about what special people the caretakers are. How giving, loving, dedicated and selfless they are. I know sleep may be difficult for some of them to achieve, at times. When sleep and rest do engulf them, I like to think angels soothe them and allow slumber to renew their souls.

My dear friend has now moved on to a new life, one we can only dream about. He left a loving family, friends who loved him and a wealth of memories and legacy for us to remember him by. His life enriched others because of his integrity, love of family and friends, encouragement, teaching, availability, laughter and warm smile. He was successful in every definition of the word.

With his good-bye to me, my life's journey has taken yet another turn. I like to think of it as my soul's journey with God. I have learned to lose any fear of moving on and seeing what is around the next bend in my road. When I take my final glance at this life I like to think he will be waiting. He will take my hand again, squeeze it gently and say, "I am glad you listened."

So am I.

ADA—At the Ten-Year Mark

The Americans with Disabilities Act is respected by many employers and gives companies guidelines for their employees who have disabilities. There most likely will always be companies and people who will look at such laws as a thorn in their side. Some have the attitude, "What makes them so special, huh?" These same people forget they could easily become part of the disabled population by a wrong turn on a road, a bullet, a fall or stroke, or any one of many causes of disability. One man I know became paraplegic during a fraternity pledge night when the young men were told to dive across the mud. My friend took them literally and *dove* and ended up with a broken neck.

No one wants this for another soul, but life has proved it is possible for anyone. Former Senator Bob Dole said it best at a ten-year

ADA celebration, "Disabilities do not show discrimination to any-one." How true.

ADA Anniversary Just One Stop On Journey

September 13, 2000

Today, I wish I had taken the bus downtown. Why? Traffic, parking and the heat, but also because I hit another car. Such is life, and no one was hurt or angry. I recalled the words I had heard about one hour prior to my accident. Former U.S. Sen. Robert J. Dole talked about how the disability progress—a movement that could be perceived as contradictory by some—is similar to the Civil Rights movement, only people with disabilities haven't been sent to the back of the bus. Many of us couldn't even get on the bus.

The Americans with Disabilities Act was put into place July 26, 1990. Ten years has passed and the act is still in its youth. Dole compared the ADA to a 10-year-old child; both having much to learn and a long way to go. Pre-ADA, it was impossible for a person using a wheelchair to get on a bus or use other public transportation. The ADA changed that and independence is more of a reality for many.

Everyone at my table during the local July event to mark ADA's anniversary was Deaf and two interpreters were "on hand" to translate the spoken work for us. Camaraderie was evident and I was inspired as we communicated freely. The word "freely" has tremendous significance for the Deaf. There was a day, not too long ago, when they would sign only in private and, I have heard, even under a table in public.

I looked around the room and realized that pre-ADA, many of the attendees most likely were restricted in personal independence and employment options. Many lives are telling improved stories today, but there is still a 70% unemployment rate among those with disabilities. There is much to do.

Dole was seated at the next table and communicated with those seated near him at our table, dispelling the myth that hearing people cannot communicate with a person who is Deaf. He was impressive, to say the least. Dole continued to meet attendees and pose with them for photographs at the conclusion of the event.

Celebrations took place all over America that day. Columbus residents were no exception and they were exceptional. One key player was Ken Campbell, ADA coordinator for the city of Columbus. His comments were sincere and informative. Mayor Michael Coleman presented him with honors for his dedication and years of work. It was personally good to see Ken again since it had been thirty-plus years since we attended Westerville High School—back when there was only one high school. This time we saw each other in a much different environment.

Mayor Coleman was gracious and warm while welcoming the honored guests and projected a positive, professional and friendly image of Columbus. His interactions with attendees emanated respect and concern. Hope Taft, Ohio's first lady at the time, announced that Gov. Bob Taft officially made July 26 Disability Awareness Day for all of Ohio and Mayor Coleman did the same for Columbus.

These people set the stage for Dole, who gave a presentation confirming his love for all people. He is a dedicated advocate for others with disabilities and wants everyone to see the person first. He made a point to say that the disability issues are strictly non-partisan—all agree on the need to make changes. His sense of humor was refreshing, creating waves of laughter. When he stated that he had been asked to take part in a celebration in Washington, D.C., but had replied, "No, I am going to Columbus, Ohio," cheers reverberated throughout the room. He was grateful his visit was not political.

We all know that for any event to play out well, many people behind the scenes must set the stage and direct the action—unfortunately too many to list here. These unnamed people skillfully planned the day and represented the following organizations: ADA-Ohio, AXIS Center for Public Awareness of People with Disabilities, Columbus Mayor's Advisory Committee on Disability Issues, Governor's Council on People with Disabilities, Ohio Developmental Disabilities Council, Ohio Rehabilitation Services Commission and Ohio Statewide Independent Living Council.

The room was filled to capacity, presenting a diverse portrait of people. People with physical and developmental disabilities were celebrating with people from businesses that sponsored the event. The support from these local businesses projected a powerful message, saying, "We see you, we hear you, and we care."

Anyone, at any time, could join this population of more than 50 million people with disabilities. No one wants that to happen, but it has and it does. As Dole stated, "Disabilities do not show discrimination to anyone." He knows this all too well.

I am also living proof, having become deaf and acquired Multiple Sclerosis. I am proud to be a part of this community of people, with satisfaction for the persons they have become despite their disabilities and possibly as a result of them. Disabilities, or special abilities, are parts of who we are.

Columbus' Dwight Lenox appropriately concluded with his heartfelt rendition of I'll Fly Away. I was overwhelmed with emotion and gratitude for the vocalist's sincerity and warmth, but also for being part of a special group of people in our community who took the time to say that they recognize each person.

As Dr. Adela A. Allen stated, "We should acknowledge differences, we should greet differences, until difference makes no difference anymore."

We are on our way, one step at a time, one smile at a time, one day at a time. See you at the bus stop.

Most people I know with disabilities aren't looking for special favors. As a matter of fact, most would prefer to flow with the mainstream with simple accommodations to be able to see a movie, hear a speech, laugh at jokes along with others, have transportation available and share lives with the people around them. They want to do these things even if it means each of them must work a little harder, ask a little louder or more often. I am part of that crowd.

Twisted Fingers

As gregarious as I am, it was surprising to me that American Sign Language made me shy. Hindsight tells me it might have been because of my desire to sign well and clearly—you know the old tapes of failure that can run again in our heads—but once I threw that old tape away, signing took on new meaning to me. Then it began to happen more naturally.

My ASL training began with Deaf Services in Worthington, Ohio. I took the beginning course where we learned finger spelling (the alphabet) and numbers. To this day, finger spelling is still my weakest part of ASL, but I keep working on it.

When my first ASL teacher showed us numbers, I quietly didn't understand the need to know numbers. I admit I didn't work diligently on numbers until the teacher had each of us ask classmates simple questions in sign, such as, "What is your phone number?" or "What is your address?" or "What time is it?" or "How old are you?" I began to reconsider my first impression and I studied.

It really *felt* like a foreign language to me, even after I had taken ASL I, II, and III. So I repeated ASL I and was fortunate enough to have a teacher, Juanita Schwartz, who did *not* speak and I took off. Also, I had a new friend who is Deaf tell me to "Just communicate."

Just communicate became my new personal motto. I was already reading lips, watching body language, utilizing e-mail and a TTY and using my residual hearing. ASL was a new addition to my list of total communication tools.

I did continue to worry, though, about how I could keep working in a hearing environment. To this end, I made an appointment at the Ohio Department of Rehabilitation to obtain advice. I met a woman, Karla, and we chatted. When we began talking about my ASL courses, I said something like, "Fingerspelling is so hard for me; I don't know if I'll ever get it. You see, my right hand is numb from MS." Karla smiled and said nothing.

My eyes watched her looking at me and I felt thoughtless for complaining. You see, Karla was born with no arms or hands, her fingers grew out from her shoulders and she could no longer walk—and she was successful and making the best of what God had given her.

I smiled sheepishly and said, "Oh my God. What is my problem? How dare I complain? No more excuses, Karla." She smiled and nodded. This was a turning point I will never forget. To this day, if my fingers get twisted when fingerspelling, I laugh, start over and sometimes jokingly slap my hand. Excuses only make me weak.

Back to School

My thirst for knowledge never seems to be quenched, so I signed up for college ASL courses, the same courses interpreters undertake, at Columbus State Community College. I knew it would be tough because most of my classmates wanted to become interpreters and were hearing. The teachers *had* to press for perfection and I was not looking to be made an exception.

When I signed up for ASL II, I was thrilled to see my teacher was Chris Evenson. She was the director of the interpreter program and we had a chance meeting a few months earlier. When we met and signed to each other, we learned we had been in high school together, she a couple years younger than I. It was a fun discovery. Now she was my teacher, but I knew intensive work was ahead of me to pass her course. I didn't want Chris to make any allowances for me simply because we knew each other.

ASL Course Lets Me Reconnect with My Past
November 22, 2000

The day my American Sign Language class at Columbus State Community College ended, I thanked the teacher, told her it had been an excellent class and was lots of fun. Much about the language was learned. So why was I feeling so sad? I gave Chris a hug and vowed to stay in touch. We gave each other a last comment in ASL to take care and we smiled. I was holding back some tears.

I walked to my car on this cool, sunny day and headed for home. The weather reminded me of the September school days I remembered from my youth. In my ASL final, Chris and I asked each other questions. One was, "How old were you when you first rode a school bus?" and she answered, "15 years old."

She explained how she lived close to school, so she walked and loved it. I replied that I, too, had lived very close to school and walked. Memories of the sound of crunching leaves underfoot rushed into my head.

Last year, Chris and I were chatting, with our hands, about ourselves and I told her I grew up in Westerville. She asked me what year I graduated; 1969, I replied.

"What?" she said. "I graduated in 1971. Did we know each other then? What was your maiden name?" Women have this dilemma at times.

"Day, what was yours?" Her maiden name was Raimonde. We both were stunned, for we knew each other in school and had been involved together in drama. She was working behind the scenes while I was on stage in Showboat. Two years later she starred in Wait Until

Dark, but I had not seen any dramas after graduation. Had 31 years really gone by that fast?

I could picture her so easily as the tiny, dark-haired "brain": that is what we called whiz kids in my day. She was someone I could never measure up to scholastically. Both our faces were beaming with good memories. That night, I pulled my musty yearbook off the shelf and confirmed my memory was correct. Then I looked at my picture and wondered how people remember me.

Now, 31 years later, Chris is my teacher, an excellent one with many skills in language and with people. I had become deaf and she had become an ASL teacher. Was it a coincidence, or not? I have found it a small treasure in my life.

Several times, I have tried to reconnect with people from school. Westerville was very small during the '50s and '60s. Many of my fellow graduates in 1969 started school with me in a kindergarten class that was held in the basement of the Masonic Temple on State Street. My attempts, at that point, had been fruitless. Now I happen to reconnect with someone from high school; we still have something in common and are friends.

After all the years, it is pleasant to be remembered and to remember. It may be selective memory but, nonetheless, I remember. I was hard of hearing then, not deaf; my hearing loss was discovered in elementary school. I was a good student in music but nothing else. That continued into my college days. It took me years to realize that when the teachers turned toward the blackboard to write, they must have continued talking to the class. I can remember more than once feeling in a haze because my classmates seemed to understand and I was lost.

I was too embarrassed to ask for clarification, fearful of appearing as dense as I was feeling. Therefore, all my energy and time was put into drama and music.

Later, I was a college student again. Times had changed, choices had increased, and I was a distance student with Ohio University. I was enrolled in the Independent Study Program and worked at my own pace. I used snail mail and finished my Junior year of college. Funny, when I was in high school, I felt at a distance. Graduation day meant I had survived and somehow earned a diploma.

I had no idea what I wanted to do with my life and everyone kept asking that infamous question, "What are you going to do?" All I really knew was music, so I studied hoping to be an elementary school music teacher. It was probably a good thing I didn't make it, but maybe the students would love a deaf music teacher? I'll never know.

Now schools have proficiency tests. To this day, tests make my stomach knot. However, today as Chris and I sat facing each other, using ASL, smiling and laughing, I finally found a test that relaxed me and made me feel good about myself. I am far from perfect at it and will continue to learn throughout my life. But for now, I feel successful. A hurdle has been overcome.

Chris had much to do with that measure of success and this is probably why the tears are on the edge of my eyes, even now, as I write. I am feeling the passing of time, the wonder of how God guides us and brings our lives to fulfillment. When I started learning ASL, I wondered if I would ever "get it." Old tapes were playing of my school days and poor grades. So I discarded those tapes and traded them in for a new CD.

Now I can remember, with a smile, walking to school and rustling through the leaves. And I remember my recent feeling of accomplishment that took only 31 years to come to fruition. Thanks, Chris.

Mouth Wide Open

My parents told me I was born with my mouth wide open and crying, like most babies. But over the years, after I learned to talk, my mouth stayed open talking away. I loved meeting new people, visiting neighbors, singing, laughing and this remains a part of me today.

It follows that, twenty-three years later, my baby, Mary, was born crying, healthy and loving to talk like her mother. When Mary was about the same age as I was when she was born, her family began to grow with three children in five years. She and her daughter, Elizabeth, love to chatter, read out loud, sing and both learned to play violin. We joke that the love of talking must be hereditary.

My hearing was getting profoundly worse as my grandchildren were being born. At one point, Mary began teaching her children Baby Sign. Her reasoning? "I always want them to be able to talk with their Nana." My heart pounded with love and appreciation.

Real Communication Takes Real Effort

July 11, 2001

We must be born with a desire to communicate. The first thing we do is open our mouths and cry out. Maybe we are saying, "Put me back where I am safe!" We'll never know.

Next we learn to babble, sit up, crawl, stand, talk and walk. If we don't talk, somehow we learn to let mom and dad know what we want or need. If we are born deaf, we use our hands to communicate long before a hearing baby makes sense of complicated verbal language. So how did that desire to connect with others evolve into some of the forms of communication prevalent today?

One day, I was having lunch at a local restaurant and watched two young children playing with toy cellular phones—at least I hoped they were toys. Another time, I was traveling via airplane and a man sat next to me talking incessantly on his tiny cell phone. It was hard to ignore and he seemed to be negotiating a business deal, yet he did all the talking. I wondered how successful that deal was since he did very little listening.

Looking around, while my little hearing dog was sleeping in my lap, a woman circled the airport lobby area talking on her cell phone while her young daughter tugged at her blouse for attention. She didn't get it. Another woman was talking while eating a meal. A man walked by with his hand up to his ear with his mini cell phone. Another young man opened a briefcase and started talking on his phone. At least six people were talking on phones in the small waiting area.

What did we do before cell phones and electronic mail? Slipping into extinction are pay phones, hand-written letters and postcards, pagers and even wonderful reunions where we finally had the opportunity to talk to someone face-to-face. I always carry quarters for pay phones when traveling. Pay phones now are usually vacant since most people talk on cell phones. There are times that cell phones must be a blessing, but who are these people talking to?

E-mail is a great time saver and communication tool, yet I would never use e-mail to discuss at length employment or personal issues. I think it is too impersonal and others cannot hear the inflection in voices or see facial expression. I opt for personal communication so emotions can be seen.

My daughter Mary, my granddaughter Elizabeth, and me.

A few months back, another issue of communication was brought to my attention when I interviewed Parker Greene, then a New Albany High School junior. My first and lasting impression was that she is a bright, intelligent, beautiful young woman who is very communicative using voice and American Sign Language. I also use both when appropriate. I learned she had her cochlear implant at age 6 and since then has had three new and improved voice processors. Her speech was clear for someone born deaf and her desire to befriend classmates was strong.

She moved to New Albany during fifth grade. She still attended Columbus Public Schools classes for the hearing impaired, where the classes were small and teachers were trained to work with children with hearing loss. In seventh grade, she attended New Albany schools where she has continued through high school. She has worked avidly to inform classmates she can hear with her cochlear implant, and she can read lips, but to little avail. Students still shy away from speaking with her.

Parker said she is lonely during her school days—although she has many close friends outside of school. Do these same students pick up their cell phones to chat incessantly with friends about basically nothing of intrinsic value? My guess is they do. But it costs nothing but a little bit of time to approach Parker and say, "Hi, how are you?" She would be more than willing to give clues on how to communicate best.

What has happened to face-to-face talk today? That is all you need to do with Parker or anyone with a hearing loss. It is courteous to face people when we talk, whether or not they can hear. We go to great lengths to learn how to use cell phones and many forms of technology. It is a much simpler and less time-consuming task to talk to other people and figure out the best way to communicate.

There are too many lonely people waiting for the international language of all human beings—a smile, a helping hand, or an attempt to communicate in a way all can enjoy life more. Take down those cell phones from your ears more often. Look others in the eye and sincerely listen for the response to your "How are you?" questions. People like Parker will smile and friendships can be born. We then can stop screaming silently within a loneliness no one should endure.

Obstacles

We all have them, the forces in life that can keep us from moving on. Whether physical or emotional, obstacles come in all shapes and sizes. Each of us has our own list. What we do or how we react to those complications can make or break the situation.

On a trip home from rainy Boston, I was stuck at Logan Airport for the night and was traveling with two others with hearing loss. Things were not going well among the three of us, and I was frustrated because of more than being stuck in Boston. When I began to write about my memory of this night, it began in anger and, thankfully, transformed into a reflection on the best part of an eventful night.

Reading to my grandchildren.

Communication Obstacles Come in Many Forms

November 4, 1998

Rain had been falling from thick clouds for days. Boston was awash. Roads had been closed and delays in all travel had become commonplace. By the time I was to return home, this was becoming old news and I was confident I could get home to Columbus. Wrong.

I am profoundly hard of hearing and traveling poses hazards that test all my creative communication skills. Waiting for my flight at the airport, and after many delays were posted, it became clear I was going to be stuck in Boston all night. I searched for a TTY (text telephone) to call home but found none. When I inquired, I was met with blank looks. OK, I was on my own.

I stood in line with the other weary travelers and waited on a regular phone. While mapping my strategy, my turn came up. I watched as a woman stood by a phone staring into the palm of her hand. I finally asked, "Are you finished?" Her face was tear-stained as she looked at me holding out the few coins in her hand. I offered her change. She spoke steadily and with emotion saying, "No, thank you. I am French. I do not know how to do this."

Suddenly I felt a kinship with this woman. With her heavy accent and my poor hearing, I quickly surmised I was not her answer. I asked her to wait while I got help. I turned and recognized another woman I remembered watching as I had conversed in sign language with a fellow traveler. I asked if she could help this woman. She had overheard and seemed to understand the situation. Her face lit up with a smile as she said, "I would be glad to help."

She, too, was a traveler from another country. Three tired and frustrated women in a foreign country (me in the hearing world) yet in a few brief moments, we had overcome any obstacles in communication. I was encouraged. Maybe you feel like the traveler from France, moving through your days lost or unsure of the language or culture; unsure of whom and how to ask for help. It is exhausting, at times, and challenging at others.

I have told my family that, as my hearing faded, it was like asking them to move to France and learn a new language. They don't complain and we get through, day by day. Being a hard of hearing or deaf traveler is very challenging and fraught with potential hazards. They are not insurmountable, they test creativity. I believe we must remember that there are many conditions and life circumstances that are not visible that people are coping with daily. Then we may not become myopic, thinking we are the only travelers. We need each other, at times more than we may know.

Is it you standing with a few coins in your hand thinking there are no resources for help? No answers? Or maybe you don't know who to ask, what to ask or how to ask? I have been there. I have been standing alone, holding out my hand and wondering why life had to be so complicated. Wondering what language these people were speaking and wondering when help would arrive.

Whatever might be causing you to feel alone, or isolated, I urge you to seek answers. There are others who know your language or want to learn. None of us truly need to stand alone. How difficult it must have been for the woman from France to ask for help in a language not her own. But she did and help arrived. You are not alone.

When Batteries Die

As recently as 2002, I would tell people I was deaf without my hearing aids. Now, with my cochlear implant, I say, "With my device on, I hear and understand about 95 percent of everything spoken and know what most sounds are. But when the batteries die, or I take the device off, I am still deaf."

The CI fascinates people. Some wonder if I have a hole in my scalp for the device to hold on to the exterior (a visual that sends me to a chair to sit and not faint). I have a magnet inside my scalp that is permanent. When I put the voice processor on, it attaches to my scalp by a magnet. When I worked in a school, I made the children laugh when I would take the piece off my ear and let it dangle in mid-air from the magnet.

All the years I spent explaining hearing loss to hearing people was a great training ground for explaining my implant and how it works. People are amazed I hear as well as I do. I stand amazed to this day as well.

Unplugged Vacuum Doesn't Do the Job

January 26, 2000

All three of our children are grown to adulthood, two with children of their own. Not too long ago our youngest daughter, Mary, and son, Michael were visiting. It was confession time. Uh-oh . . . what were we going to hear? Mary confessed that she hated vacuuming when she was younger. OK, I thought, I don't like it either. She went on to say that when it was her chore for the week, she used to run the vacuum without turning it on. But the tracks from the vacuum showed.

We laughed and I said it must have been harder to vacuum with it turned off. She agreed. Other childhood confessions followed. Somehow, we all survived. Recently, I was reflecting on this confession time, glad our children realize the "error of their ways." We, as parents, were far from perfect as well. That's probably why our family stays close. We love each other in spite of our imperfections.

How often do we make life harder than it needs to be? We struggle to push the unplugged vacuum across the rug. All the outward signs of a finished job are evident, but the job is not completed. We work twice as hard as we need to. It is a human condition. The "signs" are all on the surface. The dirt and dust remain in the carpet. In our souls.

For many years I pushed ahead pretending that I could hear, pretending to understand. Why? Now it's confession time for me, only this is very public. I wanted to be thought of as "normal," "average," "the same as everyone else." I didn't want to stand out as peculiar. Now I look on the word peculiar as unique; an individual. I like it and am comfortable being unique.

I also cope with another invisible condition, Multiple Sclerosis. Some time ago I asked my doctor why I had all these weird problems. "You are not weird, you are unique," he stated. I remember laughing. I was still pushing, in those days. I have stopped pushing to be the world's version of normal. It is impossible for me to fit into any mold.

A couple of summers ago, I was asked to sign some of my poetry at Deaf Poetry in the Park. I was so nervous. Would the Deaf accept me because I was not born Deaf? Would my hard of hearing friends think

I had abandoned them for the Deaf world? Would anyone understand what my poetry meant? Would my signing be OK? I fretted so.

Then I received an e-mail from a friend, Pat Vincent, who quoted a famous person. He said, "Liz, all I can say is a quote from Popeye: 'I yam what I yam and that's all that I yam' and 'Be just what you is, not what you is not. Folks such as this is the happiest lot.'" He went on to say, "Just be yourself and don't worry about what others think."

That was tough, since I was just learning who "myself" was: "Too soon old, too late smart." But when I got up to sign, I thought, "I yam what I yam," turned my hearing aids off, glanced at my smiling husband and went to it. Lori, one of my American Sign Language teachers was there and loved it.

Being late-in-life deafened is a world in between culturally Deaf and hearing. It's difficult to define. Still, I feel comfortable in this world of somewhere in between. I have stopped pushing my proverbial unplugged vacuum across the floor. I have decided to enjoy life more, stop worrying about what others think of me and move on. How we deal with our life circumstance is our choice. I like to find the humor in situations related to my hidden conditions.

While watching the space shuttle lift off some time ago, with John Glenn [then in his 70's] on board, I asked a person my age if in 30 years he would go into space. He said, "yes," but I said I didn't think I would.

"But you could go to bars!" I thought he said. I hesitated, thinking he could not have said that. I smiled, he looked confused and then it hit me—"Oh you said we could go to Mars." He asked what I thought he had said and when I told him, we both laughed heartily. With humor, people feel more comfortable asking me questions.

I know my daughter plugs in the vacuum now. I am quite sure she still does not like it. I will be working for the completion of my life practicing the "life of my heart," to focus on the awesome uniqueness of each of God's creatures, to develop my soul and spirit. I will never be a hearing person or physically graceful. But I have many other abilities. Accepting this allows me to move on, to do the best I can every day of my life. And all the while I try to keep this quote in mind (with apologies to English teachers and editors): "Be just what you is, not what you is not."

Somewhere in Between

March 15, 1997

Not a true member of the hearing world now,
Not born into the Deaf one.
So I am somewhere in between
But not a world that is unseen.
As the years have flown by
My hearing lagged behind.
Sometimes people were not very kind,
But through it all I had to learn
What others thought and their not meaning to spurn.
So my opinion, for awhile, of myself
Was somewhere hidden on a shelf,
Until I decided to accept
And not worry if others were to reject.
Usually others just need to know
What I require and so now I show,
I hope, with kindness, what I need to know
To communicate best in this world here below.
For Heaven above us and all around
Never takes heed if we make a sound
If we talk with our hands and treat others with love
God will bless it and help us understand.
So, I just do my best every day of my life
Whether speaking or signing or staying up late to write.
For I am somewhere in between and now I know
Being somewhere is something and
Now others I can show.

Being what I was at this time in my life was a challenge. Many thoughts flew through my brain about what I should do with my life. Was it time to shift careers? Go back to school? Retreat? I had no clue. I also knew that only I could solve the puzzle as it was, and is, my life. I believe that each life is a gift from God, and I was not about to waste mine.

Worship "Normally"

My next step seemed obvious but difficult. I knew I would be deaf within a few years and cochlear implants seemed foreign to me. My next step was to knock on the door of Holy Cross Lutheran Church for the Deaf. You heard me, *knock*. I felt like a fool. I saw people standing in the pastor's office on this Saturday and knocked. Why didn't they respond? I was so ingrained in the hearing world my brain had not shifted gears.

Ah! Someone saw me in the window. Here she comes. I proceeded to use my rustic sign language to ask what time services were on Sundays. These people were patient and must have sensed my dilemma. Later I would learn there was a buzzer at the door that activated a light in the pastor's office. I knew I had much to learn.

Bob and I attended church services at Holy Cross the next day. The first question everyone asked was, "You Deaf? Hearing? Which?" and using my simplest sign, I responded I was hard of hearing and deaf without my hearing aids. We were both received with smiles and hugs. I was astounded and pleased. Bob seemed comfortable, too. He and I only had a personal sign system at this point, so we waited to discuss details later.

The service began and, yes, it was different, but I liked it. No one seemed to be watching Bob or me. Worship was the order of the morning and we joined in. Then Pastor Ed Bergstresser, of Grove City, stood to preach and I found myself smiling. He spoke and signed. Up until now, this has been the best communication atmosphere for me: speaking and signing. Now I knew Bob could enjoy the service with me and I was really pleased.

Pastor Ed's sermons were uplifting and we continued to attend Holy Cross for more than a year. I took part in a few things at the church and began to understand the Deaf culture with a new respect. There were particular people who seemed to take me under their wings, teach and befriend me. One woman saw me at a Deaf Services fundraising event outside the church and she asked *me* to assist *her*. I felt honored. It was simple enough; she wanted me to ask the bartender for lemon in her water using my voice. The connection continued between worlds for me.

Many of the members who were in their older years used finger spelling almost exclusively and I found it hard to follow. These same people were patient and would smile. I never pretended I understood and would apologize for my inability to read finger spelling. Over this year, though, I improved and became more comfortable using sign language. I learned, through this experience, that people were glad I was working so hard at communicating. I know I messed up more than once and no one seemed to mind. I felt accepted and loved.

During our time participating in worship at Holy Cross, prayer and praise took on new meaning for me. One Sunday as I signed the Lord's Prayer, when I came to the part where we sign or say, ". . . and forgive us our sins as we forgive others who sin against us." I dropped my arms and stood in amazement. It was an epiphany, or revelation, for me. I realized at that moment that if God forgives me all my sins, I should be able forgive others who have wronged me. I also understood I cannot do that on my own power but through God's grace. I wondered why I never heard the Lord's Prayer in that way and realized that using my hands and arms sealed the message in my heart. When I think of it that way, I can say that my eyes were opened to new meaning of forgiveness. When our daughter, Mary, was in Catholic high school, she loved the religion classes and even crossing herself after prayer. She told me, "It's like sealing the prayer in my heart." When she had said that, I was touched deeply. This day I finally understood what she meant. I talked to her about it months later and she understood, too.

Now I knew I could worship if I became completely deaf and I felt myself relaxing about my life choices. I felt accepted and attended a few Deaf club events outside the church. I was asked to speak at a Deaf club dinner. I was too nervous to sign and asked for an interpreter. Many of my newer friends were in the audience and several of my ASL teachers. Yet I felt it was more a sign of respect to have an interpreter than to stumble through my presentation. It was a good choice.

During this same time frame, I was President of the local SHHH chapter and was moving from the hearing world, through the hard of hearing world to the Deaf world. This experience helped me learn how to switch from using speech and moving right into using sign. It became more natural. To this day, I still prefer to sign the Lord's Prayer rather than speaking it. Even when I pray alone, I find myself signing prayers and songs, even if only in my mind.

After attending Holy Cross for nearly a year, I began to feel Bob was missing our home church at the time, Gethsemane Lutheran, and suggested we go to services there for awhile. This church had added an FM listening system, top of the line, for people with hearing loss, before we ever attended Holy Cross. It was helping me then so I tried it a year later and got nothing.

I admit I was sad. I wanted to hear, even if it was parts of what was being said. But I got nothing. The choir music must have been beautiful, and I used to be part of that same choir, but I only heard bits and pieces, so it sounded distorted to me. Again, I was sad. I missed music terribly.

When we left, Bob filled me in on the sermon content and announcements. He knew I was sad because my face is a tell-all kind of face. I don't hide emotions very well.

People at Gethsemane understood our predicament. Many knew I was deaf without my hearing aids. They had seen the children's choir sign Silent Night and the Lord's Prayer under my direction. Their kindnesses and tender-hearted understanding made my emotions move like riding a roller coaster because I wanted to be a part of this congregation in a more meaningful way.

We felt stuck in between the hearing and Deaf worlds. Both of us this time. I was having a hard time "enjoying" worship at Holy Cross since Bob could hear, and he felt worship difficult at Gethsemane because I could not hear. We made a choice to worship privately for awhile. It was all we knew to do. We stayed in touch with our Deaf and hearing friends to a small degree and stayed home on Sundays. We made Sunday mornings our moment for quiet time together. We often took walks, read the paper, sat on our porch or sipped coffee. All our senses told us God understood since He knows our hearts.

What Is Normal?

During this same time, my MS seemed to be worsening. I was learning about how my body reacts and what it needs during times when the disease was active. Fatigue was common, especially for me as a reporter who sometimes had to drive hundreds of miles a month. Exhaustion also affects emotions and clear thinking. But I found in my fatigue a new clarity of thinking. I learned to pace myself better.

The word "normal" has baffled me for years. How do you define it?

Don't Be So Quick to Define "Normal"

Early 2002

Please define "normal." The American Heritage Dictionary defines the word as "Conforming to a norm or standard, typical," or "of average intelligence or development, free from physical or emotional disorder," or "the usual state or amount."

Words such as normal and average should be left to statistical analysis, not used with human conditions. I have never been normal. As a youth, I wanted so much to be like everyone else, yet I always felt I was in left field and not quite sure why. Maybe my hearing loss, discovered in fourth grade, put me in situations where I didn't quite get it and didn't even know what I was missing. This is a likely scenario. Looking back, however, many children probably felt the same way and, like me, thought they were alone. I have come to terms with my lack of hearing. But I often am stunned by my inability to walk normally—there's that word again.

When I was a child and young adult, I practically lived outside. I could be found on my bicycle or roller skates, running and swimming and doing all that was possible in a given day. Now, because of the onset of multiple sclerosis which reared its head more than 30 years ago, walking my dog around the block is a challenge. My legs weaken easily and do what I call "flopping." Walking has become frustrating for me.

This [same] year I caved in and started using the motor scooters provided by grocery stores, because my husband and I love to wander and just look. Often we go in different directions and will temporarily lose one another. Before relying on the scooters, I would almost be in tears trying to find him while my legs flopped. So I drive. I love it, I spend more money and don't go home needing a nap to recuperate.

But I look normal, people tell me. There is that word again. Yes, I don't have any obvious or visual indications of my hearing loss, but I didn't hide my hearing aids. I use a cane only when I need to—it's only one more thing to carry—and I've been told I don't look old enough to use a scooter. So I get funny stares and glares from strangers as I motor through the store. I don't mind when kids are staring—they're wonderful and I guess they're thinking they want to join me. I joke with them. Some people move out of my way. I tell them "I'm not going to run you down," hoping a little humor will minimize my difference and have them see me instead of the scooter.

Recently I interviewed Barbara, a woman who has become blind. She said it can be a lonely life because people don't feel comfortable striking up a conversation. But her dog, Bevy, helps bridge that gap. The beautiful golden retriever kept her head in my lap during the entire interview, though she was never far from her owner.

Throughout the years, I have written several columns explaining how I believe everyone has something with which they must learn to live. I firmly believe this. It may be physical, spiritual, emotional or intellectual. But none of us is perfect. Perfect is another word I try to use sparingly. Perfect compared to what? How can we talk about normal, perfect or average without excluding people's feelings?

When people say to me that I look normal, I have learned to say in response, "Oh, I hope not because I can't define that word. Can you?" It used to be "normal" for me to walk and hear without help, without hearing aids, canes, motor scooters and closed captioning. No longer. I must adapt to the new me so others can do the same thing.

It's tough. I still dream of running down stairs and hearing everything without wearing hearing aids. Those dreams are healthy and I love them. But reality smacks me in the face upon wakening. Do I cry? Sometimes. How do I cope? Day by day, minute by minute, hug by hug from my husband, children, grandchildren and friends.

What do I hope for? That others will continue to see me, or see Barbara and the millions who must go the extra mile to get where they are going. We seek common courtesy and respect. Please don't preconceive limitations. Our bodies are already doing that for us and we work twice as hard to do what many do naturally. You never know when it might be you having to go that extra mile, though I don't wish that on anyone. If you strike up a conversation with Barbara, believe me, you will laugh. She does stand-up comedy and she is hilarious.

Talk with me, too, and you never know when I might write a story about you. People fascinate me. I hear beyond words by listening intently and watching. As I scoot, or maybe stumble, past you, just say hello. If I fall, please help me up and I will try to do the same for you.

As a reporter with MS and deafness, I had unique challenges to overcome. Much of the challenge came from other people who wanted to use my deafness to their benefit: to hide facts or say I had facts or quotes incorrect. I always followed up and double checked everything. I am not saying I never made mistakes, because I am human and did. But my check system was strong and after I got my CI, I must have scared these same people with my ability to finally hear clearly.

My editor, Martin Rozenman, always stood beside me and taught me. He understood both sides of the situation and did not want me to fail. This attitude toward me kept me moving forward and searching for ways to improve communication.

Mickey Mouse Voices

April 22, 2002 is a date that is etched in my brain—literally. This is the day Dr. Darryl Willett with OhioENTSurgeons performed a miracle in my head. He put a cochlear implant in my right cochlea and under my scalp at Grant-Riverside Hospital in Columbus, Ohio.

This date was also our wedding anniversary and we found the perfect way to celebrate. I wrote this about two weeks after my surgery and two weeks prior to the activation of the implant. I'll leave it in the tense it was written in so the emotions at that time will come through strong. We all know that things *did* change and my device *was* programmed two weeks later. This is how I felt at the time of writing.

> ### *We Have New Reason to Celebrate Anniversary*
>
> May 15, 2002
>
> April 22 was our 24th wedding anniversary, but I slept through most of it. Bob, my husband, understood. This same day I had cochlear implant surgery at Grant-Riverside Hospital under the skilled care of surgeon Dr. Darryl Willett.

148

It is an anniversary Bob and I won't forget—the day I went bionic. Our lives will change again in less than a month. I will have had the stitches removed, and my external hearing device will be programmed and activated to work with the device implanted in the cochlea of my right inner ear and under my scalp. No more hearing aids, which have been such a blessing in my life.

Hearing the implant work will be nothing short of another miracle in my life. My ability to hear had only one way to go—up. The prognosis is excellent. Dr. Willett tested the device during surgery and it worked. My brain responded and soon I will hear better and differently. Time will tell how well.

A new phase in my life and in the lives of everyone who knows me has begun. Yes, I have some pain and discomfort for now, but I never felt alone. I turned my life over to God years ago and must trust in this act of faith over and over throughout my life. My life was literally in the hands of the surgeon and other medical professionals. They met with obstacles—which included a herniated nerve and a narrow passageway—to perform the miraculous implant procedure.

Friends, family, coworkers and even strangers prayed and supported both of us through the process. As Bob anxiously awaited the end of my surgery, which was supposed to last a few hours, he became more anxious knowing anything could happen and he had no control. That's tough for some people and he is one of them.

It helped when Bob met Amy Erickson, of Upper Arlington, who was volunteering this day at the hospital waiting room. During a few conversations, Amy figured out that I was the reporter whom she had been e-mailing ideas for library stories, yet we had not met. Bob got a kick out of the coincidence and she reassured Bob and did what she could to reunite us quickly.

Prior to surgery, I repeatedly said to Bob, "All I want is to see your face when I wake up." When Dr. Willett realized I was not responding to anyone in recovery even though I was awake, he broke protocol and requested Bob come see me. Bob, who remembered my wish, took my hand and I told him I was thirsty. He fed me ice chips and I said they tasted like candy to my sore throat.

The nurses and doctor stood back, prompting Bob to ask me—I read his lips and he used sign language because I was totally deaf—to raise my eyebrows, pucker my lips, smile and blink. They needed to know if my facial nerves were intact; everything was fine. All I cared about was that Bob was there with me. I would have danced if possible.

Bob and I gave each other the perfect anniversary gift, but the first we could talk about this was four nights after my surgery. I had been too squeamish to hear details prior to then. Bob told me about the surgery as described to him by Dr. Willett and I realized how blessed I was throughout the ordeal. The greatest gift we could possibly share, on any day, became real when hindsight showed us I truly was waiting for him in the recovery room. I don't remember anything until the moment when I saw his face. I responded and he knew how to reach me at my emotional level and in silence.

We had no fear. I know I wasn't a pretty sight with my tubes and bandages, but Bob really didn't care about anything except our being together. I had to pry my wedding band off my finger because of the massive fluids puffing my entire body up like a balloon. But two days later I began to deflate. I put the ring back on and said, "For better or worse, richer or poorer—we have had it all now and the ring stays on."

Our gift to each other was not tangible, but we can carry it continually. It is hard to believe love gets stronger when it is already bonded and blessed by God. But it does. Bob has seen me at my worst and best and I too have seen him at his highs and lows. Our marriage vows could include, "In puffiness or slimness . . . we are glued together for eternity, yet are two separate souls giving and taking continually from each other's lives, blessing each other, learning to lean a bit on each other, learning to laugh even when it hurts, and gently cleansing each other's wounds—physical, emotional and spiritual."

We must treasure this gift as life itself. Life is tenuous and all too short, but as Bob and I have been reminded, it is so worth living.

And the news story followed soon after.

A Journey Back to Hearing

Reporter Liz Thompson's Cochlear Implant Restores Sounds

July 24, 2002

My 50-year journey into deafness was filled with defeat and triumph. My return to the world of sound is remarkable—a technological miracle.

My hearing loss began as a young girl in elementary school. I taught myself to lip read and watch body language. At 39 I got my first hearing aid and realized how much I had been missing. The last 10 years my hearing declined rapidly to deafness.

The return to hearing began when I failed a test on January 8, 2002. I went to OhioENTSurgeons for my annual hearing test. My ears and brain failed me. I understood only 8 percent of the words spoken in my left ear—without hearing aids—and repeated none correctly listening with my right ear. Laura Anderson, an audiologist from northwest Columbus, gave me the news: I was a candidate for a cochlear implant.

The most common type of deafness is caused by damaged hair cells in the cochlea, the hearing part of the inner ear. The 15,000 hair cells can be destroyed by many things, including infection, trauma, loud noise, aging or birth defects.

The implant is a surgical treatment that works like an artificial human cochlea, helping to send sound from the ear to the brain. The array implanted in my cochlea has 22 electrodes that stimulate the hair cells so my brain can perceive sound. The surgeon works for two to four hours on one ear to implant the array and a receiver-stimulator device under the scalp that also contains a magnet which connects with an exterior magnet.

Questions and Answers

My audiologist, Laura Anderson, audiologist Beth Fais and Dr. Darryl Willett, who would perform the surgery, jumped into action. They anticipated my questions and gave me visuals of the implant device.

Willett warned me he would have to shave part of my hair. I didn't care if he had to shave my whole head if it meant I could hear. He also said that after surgery I would be in the hospital for up to 24 hours for observation.

I was not deterred. I wanted to get going, to have any preliminary tests done, to go for it now. I told Willett I wanted the surgery "yesterday." The required CAT scan proved hopeful. I felt my care was in good hands. Willett's infectious smile, energy and skill were a comfort to Bob and me throughout the entire process. That confidence grew when the final tests by Dr. John Krupko's Westerville Clinic were completed.

The insurance signoff proved lengthy, likely because the final billing would total more than $70,000 for devices, hospital stay, surgery, recovery and continued care with OhioENTSurgeons. It amazed me when I saw the break down of the billing. Dr. Willett got less than $4,000 for the surgery, $20 for a pill I never took, and the cost of each test. It was worth every penny but I had wished it cost much less.

Surgery Day

Surgery went well but longer than anticipated. Even with the preliminary tests, Willett said later that until he's in surgery he is not sure exactly what he will have to deal with. The area where he drilled narrowed to the size of a pencil tip and he had to redirect where he would put the under-the-scalp device before he could insert the implant in the cochlea of my inner ear. He drilled next to the facial nerve and told Bob later that he was concerned the heat from the drill could affect the delicate facial nerve. It did not. His skill again proved worthy.

Medical advances give the surgeon the ability to test the implant before finishing surgery. My implant worked, my brain responded to its signal. I would be told later they knew the implant would work, but how well we wouldn't know for another month.

Recovery Process

The hospital stay was overnight and my head felt huge from the massive gauze bandage, but I had no post-surgery side effects. I would be remiss if I did not report the excellent care given me at Grant-Riverside Hospital.

It was six weeks later that I learned the full names of the nurses and techs who cared for me making sure their names were in the newspaper as a way of thanking them. My nurses were Lilly Peng, Christie Crabb, Tove Albert, Darci McNeilly, and techs Tracy Wollfolk and Sara Schaedler who went above and beyond.

I was totally deaf and recuperating from surgery, not always the best of communication circumstances. These women wrote everything down for me from instructions to words of encouragement. This took extra time yet the women never appeared bothered. They had to wake me often through the night to check my low blood pressure and temperature. Each one woke me by taking my right arm and tapping it gently until I awoke so I would not be startled. My silent hospital stay held no trauma.

Once home, I would not sleep lying down until the fourth night after surgery. I became such good friends with Bob's recliner I begged for one of my own.

For one month we all waited, prayed and hoped for the best as I healed.

Exactly one month after surgery, May 22, my device was programmed, called mapping, by my audiologist, Laura Anderson, as Bob and my parents, Jim and Mary Day of Westerville, waited with me. Laura activated it and asked me if I could hear her. I thought the computer was going crazy with all the odd noise. When I said, "What's wrong with the computer?" I realized I heard my voice.

Sounds Everywhere

Everyone sounded like Mickey Mouse talking under water, but that sounded wonderful nonetheless. I could understand every word even though it was a detached sound. My range of hearing high and low pitches was wide, which I was told was excellent. Laura told me it was to be my worst day of hearing, and I would notice improvements over the coming months. That night I heard everything I could. I went through the house and outside just listening and laughing.

In the next two months I would hear, for the first time or since early childhood: laughter clear and strong and in different pitches, my voice, water going down the drain, a crow cawing, all kinds of birds, jets flying overhead, the wind and leaves rustling—I really missed that sound—voices on the radio and words to old songs, turn signals, conversations in public, computer keys tapping, mine and everyone else typing at work. It's a busy place.

There was ice clinking in a glass, Bob yawning, the dogs panting, the fish tank bubbling, doors clicking shut, rings on my hands hitting the banister on the stairs, microwave buttons and my Aunt Eva's soft, Southern accent.

I am learning to hear again, and learning to trust what I hear. With a simple device, I can talk on the telephone with ease. Later I may not need the device.

I had given up music and had given my guitar to my daughter, Mary. I bought a new one and as I work on calluses, I delight with

> every strum. The friend I said good-bye to so many years ago is home again.
>
> It was true in a different way for my husband. "It's good to have you back," Bob said.
>
> It is good to be here.

The story tells most of what activation day was like for me. It was amazing and I could not stop laughing with sheer joy. Drs. Willett and Howard Lowery, who first comprehensively diagnosed my hearing loss at age twenty-nine, were beckoned to join the celebration of hearing. Dr. Willett hugged me and Dr. Lowery beamed with joy in his usual fashion. Dr. Lowery performed the first cochlear implant in Franklin County, Ohio, in the mid-1970s. He had seen many advances and other patients with a new ability to hear.

All the audiologists came to the room as Timary Skaggs, *SNP* photographer, moved between people taking photos. She, too, was thrilled, as she and I had worked together numerous times. I had wanted my parents to come to activation day because I wanted them to hear professionals say I'm deaf so they might finally understand. I'm glad they were there to experience the thrill of my hearing returning.

Bob needed to return to work and my parents drove home. I was to drive home alone and Bob warned me of all the sounds I might hear and be startled by. Of course, no one knew how I would react to new sounds and driving could have been hazardous. It was not. I thrilled at every sound from the turn signal, car horns blowing, people's voices on the radio, and my own voice as I commented on what I was hearing.

It was a breezy, warm day with a thunderstorm looming in the distance. My first action, after greeting my dogs, was to go outside and listen. I had missed nature sounds more than anything—the wind, bird songs, leaves—everything. The first sound I heard was a jet flying very high. It took me time to find it and I was amazed I could hear this sound. The wind picked up and I watched the tree limbs moving. Was I hearing the wind and the leaves blowing? Still not sure, I watched the motion of the trees and timed it with the sound I heard. Sure enough. It was the wind. I cried with joy. All I had heard for years was the wind blowing in my hearing aids, which sounds like wind you hear blowing in an outdoor microphone.

Next I heard a crow and it sounded so loud. The rain began and I heard the patter on the roof and then the ground. I was in hearing heaven on earth. I moved inside and walked through the house listening. Snert, my dachshund, stared at me wondering what was up and then he barked; he was so loud! No wonder it bothered others when he barked incessantly. He was loud for a tiny dog.

When Bob came home, he was anxious to learn how I was doing. He was still overwhelmed knowing I could hear again and understand. We did some distance testing to see if I could hear from room to room (without walls in between) and I could. Naturally, I faced Bob and asked him to face me, as was our custom over the years. Then I laughed and asked him to turn away and say something. I got it. It was amazing.

As I heard a person's voice for the first time, each one sounded like Mickey Mouse. I asked them to keep talking and I could hear the voice turning more natural. It was like my brain remembered and the high pitches I had not heard for many years became part of the voice. But the clarity bowled me over.

Our good friend, Don Huiner, was over one evening soon after activation and I was in the kitchen, which connected openly to the family room. Bob was facing away from me talking to Don. He said something in a teasing manner about me and I said, "That's not true, Bob, and you know it." Don, Bob and I laughed and Bob said to Don, "I can't get away with anything anymore!"

I had to learn to trust what I was hearing. I was hearing without any obvious effort and I kept thinking I had to work at hearing like I had for more than thirty years. But I did not need to work, just listen and trust. I asked often, "What's that sound?" to learn it was the furnace, a fan, a horn or some such noise.

My next visit to Laura for another mapping, which happened frequently the first year, I told her it felt like I was mouthing words silently. But my voice defied that logic. She explained that I had been talking using my throat so I could *feel* my voice because I could not hear it. I was astounded and didn't realize this. No wonder my voice carried through the newsroom and the house. I was literally shouting in a guttural fashion to hear myself.

Mappings or Programming

This process is interesting and I will try to describe it. I enlisted the help of Paula Dendiu Beale, M.A., CCC-A, Audiologist, of OhioENTSurgeons, Inc. When I called her, I read my rather inane description and told her I really needed help with the words. She sent me an e-mail, which I placed in the appendix, describing all the aspects of mapping. I asked Paula if MAP or MAPPING was an acronym for something and she replied, "We have been asking that same question for twenty years."

I'm not sure why they call it a mapping but my take on it is that, using the computer to play tones, the audiologist determines what I hear and what is comfortable, from which she develops a map to my hearing ability. The first six months, I was wearing what I call the body pack or body-worn processor. The magnet stuck to my scalp and a holder went over my ear, just like a behind-the-ear hearing aid without the plastic in my ear. There is a coated wire from the holder to my voice processor, which is a little larger than a standard cell phone. It is powered by two AA rechargeable batteries. When I am getting a new mapping, the base of the processor is removed and connected to an adapter that connects directly to the computer, in my case, a laptop computer. Laura calls up my file/last mapping and presses keys to get to the place for the mapping.

Because I have tinnitus, ringing in the ears, I have requested for years that the beeps during a hearing test be in a series of three beeps.

This way I can judge whether it is a true sound or the ringing. I do that with my mappings as well. So when I hear "beep, beep, beep," I raise my hand signaling I hear it. The pitches go so low and high that it amazes me. I say to Laura, "Boy, that was way up there," and she chuckles.

I have a tendency to push to the max to get improved ability to hear. One time Laura kept saying, "Are you sure you want it that loud?" and I said I did. When she activated the new program, I fell back in my chair and laughed. "Maybe that's a little too loud?" I said smiling. "Let's go back and cut it back a little," Laura said patiently. She tirelessly works with me to get it right. My ability to perceive more sounds is still increasing, even five years later. It is amazing and fun at the same time.

Connecting

At the time of my CI activation, all three of our children were grown and off living their own lives. Our connection had been e-mail, instant messaging on the computer, the relay service, and my TTY.

Now could we talk on the phone? Hmmm . . . I was not sure about this adapter but I would give it a try and call our daughter, Mary. She has the softest voice of the three and I knew if I could hear and understand her, the device was a miracle.

Connecting with Daughter Comes Full Circle

June 2002

Hindsight offers a unique perspective. In the late '70s, I was a single parent of a preschool-aged daughter, Mary. I knew working outside the home would separate us during the day. I didn't have a choice and so I tried to make the best of the situation. Before it was called "quality time," I found ours in unusual places and times.

During these years I worked on Ohio State University's campus and began my 10-year experience at Battelle Columbus Laboratories. I enrolled Mary in nearby day-care centers and later in close, private schools. Each day I dropped her off at these schools and picked her up after work. Sometimes I met her for lunch and we would picnic at nearby parks. Nothing fancy, just a needed break. What I remember most vividly were the times in the car transporting Mary to and from schools. We moved about in my old, standard Chevy Vega, which never failed me in any weather, amazingly. Mary and I developed safe games of communication on our travels through traffic. It became "our" time and we anticipated sharing our days, even when she was very little. She's always loved to talk, just like her mother. Often I found myself shifting gears due to in-town traffic. Mary decided one day to gently put her tiny hand on top of mine. I still remember I looked at her and we both smiled. It became our time to hold hands and talk. When I wasn't shifting gears, I would take her hand and we would move in syncopation to a safe hold when I needed my hand for driving.

We shared so much during those hours. She asked me all kinds of questions; let's face it, she had a captive audience. I didn't mind. In those travels, she learned about how I didn't use bottles to feed her as a baby. We talked about how people are different and how wonderful it is to see the differences. We sang and we made up our own form of speech, which we would use while giggling for years to come. We counted cars and trucks and read license plates when she was old enough to read.

Not too long ago, she and I were talking about these days. She has similar memories, from a child's perspective, but these were special times for her, too. Communication changed for the two of us as my ability to hear diminished, so much that we could not talk on the telephone. She was married and living in California. My husband, Bob, solved the dilemma when he bought a TTY, a text telephone, for both of us so we could type our thoughts back and forth. Then e-mail became reality, followed by automatic "instant messaging," and Mary and I were able to chat frequently on the computer.

They moved to Dayton [Ohio] for four years, where we were able to visit, use sign language and speech. Her husband, also Bob, is in the Air Force and they were back in California with their three children. We missed them dearly, made worse when our communications became bungled again. My hearing had deteriorated to a point at which I was classified as deaf. But I was given the opportunity to have cochlear implant surgery shortly after their move. With a simple adapter, I can hear on the phone better than I have since my teenage years. I can understand my grandchildren and carry on conversations similar to what Mary and I had in the car years ago. The only difference now is I'm not holding their hand.

One recent Saturday, I was chatting with Mary and she apologized for not e-mailing or writing to me recently. Then we both laughed because we knew why: We were talking regularly on the phone again, similar to those days in the car. We were sharing daily adventures just as we did then, only Mary now is talking about her own children who were ages, 5, 4 and 2, at the time.

"I guess it is so much fun talking on the phone with you again, I end up having nothing new to write," she said. I agreed wholeheartedly. We laughed and she said Andrew wanted to say hello and then I heard, "Hi Nana. Hi Nana. I love you, bye."

What goes around comes around. Thank God.

Landing Upright

We moved to Phoenix, Arizona, a second time in January 2003. Finding work was not difficult like it had been in 1995, when my hearing was becoming a setback. I hated to leave my reporting job at *SNP*, but the timing seemed right for Bob's work. I was ready to try something new again and I took only good memories of *SNP* and my work with me. This was my farewell column. I knew I would miss my column writing.

I'm Ready to Land on Feet Again in Arizona
January 8, 2003

Pretending has never been a talent of mine. Saying goodbye is another asset in which I am lacking. Tears inevitably flow—publicly and privately. Now I am saying goodbye to a large, diverse and mostly unknown population—my readers.

My husband, Bob, my hearing dog, Snert, our golden retriever, Jack, and I are moving to Arizona Saturday. We plan to stay this time, and eventually retire in the Valley of the Sun. I now realize, with the marvelous hindsight, that my panic in Arizona seven years ago brought us back to Ohio for a reason. It was caused by my declining ability to hear.

I believe in writing from the heart. It is the only way I know to write and I thank God *Suburban News Publications* has allowed me to do that in some cases even as I learned to be a journalist. My editor, Marty Rozenman, was a patient and great teacher. Because of him I leave with a new understanding and respect of journalism. He always quasi-joked that I was in the Martin Rozenman School of Journalism. I call him my professor. The best I ever had.

Marty said he wanted me to begin as a stringer—a part-time, free-lance reporter—to get my feet on the ground. I thought that strange for I believed my feet were already on the ground. Now, more than two years later, I feel a jolt as I land squarely on the ground with my face to the future. My learning has been like that of a dry sponge. I have soaked up everything continually as I became grounded, more level-headed and experienced in the world of small government issues and the varied lives of the fascinating people I interviewed.

I would be remiss if I didn't thank the many people who shared their lives with me during interviews. I have seen tears and laughter, sadness, mourning and remorse, joy and triumph. These times will never be forgotten and I loved each interview for their original content and the surprises which inevitably unfolded. I was treated to beautiful music, fabulous art, great stories and tearful memories. I learned to play shuffleboard and was challenged to learn chess. I was hugged by children and adults, met kids facing the future with hope and talked with senior citizens looking back on their lives with pride. My eyes were opened.

My hope is Arizona has a writing job for me so these experiences will continue. This month marks the beginning of the sixth year I have written a column for *SNP*—first as a guest columnist, then with the standing head, "Day by Day" and now as a staff reporter. It has been more fun than words can say.

Many of you wrote letters to me, especially as I shared experiences with my hearing loss, then my cochlear implant and my new world of hearing. I rediscovered those letters today as I was packing my home office. I cherish each one and am so glad you all have been in my life and shared your thoughts with me. I'm humbled to think my words may have brightened your lives, letting you know you are not alone.

My writing was a catharsis for me coping with hearing loss and multiple sclerosis. Your letters helped affirm I was headed in the right direction. When I was very young, someone, whose name escapes me, said to be careful what you write down and write so that you would not mind anyone reading it. Good advice.

I want to thank my in-house editor, as Commentary Editor Cliff Wiltshire recently called my husband, because he has listened to more writing than any human should endure. He listened to my ideas and magically refined them to capture my meaning for my columns.

With all of this—combined with my 51 years of life experience, my new ability to hear and my love of people—I know I am headed to an uncertain but promising future. I no longer feel the panic of years gone by. I know God is leading me somewhere and I will go. Even when my unsuspecting, loud voice boomed through the newsroom and Dorothy [newsroom receptionist Dorothy Stoyer] patiently listened to my messages for me due to my severe hearing loss, I pushed forward somehow knowing it would work out in the end. It has.

These experiences have become a part of who I am. For the last time in Ohio, in print, I say to each of you:

Thanks for listening!

Having always wanted to work with children, upon arriving in Arizona, I applied for work with Deer Valley Unified School District #97 and landed a job working at a middle school with special needs children. It was rewarding and challenging for me. My learning curve jumped again and life was interesting.

Later I worked in an elementary school with teacher Cheryl Monical, who taught me to teach. She gave me experiences I had dreamed of in college—to help children learn to read and think. For this I will remain grateful.

Joel Nilsson, editor with the *Arizona Republic*, hired me in March 2003 as a community columnist. From March 2003 to May 2005, I wrote about many issues of the community I lived in—from traffic, trash, and public service to schools. I loved this experience and working with Joel.

Testing, 1 . . . 2 . . . 3

In October 2002, before we moved to Arizona in 2003, Laura Anderson, my audiologist at OhioENTSurgeons, told me I was doing so well with my implant that I qualified for a research project at Arizona State University. I contacted The Cochlear Implant Research Laboratory at Arizona State University and Michael F. Dorman, Ph.D., told me they would fly Bob and me out to Phoenix, taking care of all expenses including meals for three days, if I would spend four hours in the research lab.

I agreed, naturally, and we had a great vacation. The research was fascinating to me as I sat in a soundproof room responding to various voices from a computer and repeated the sentences. The research assistant, Tony Spahr, was easy to work with and diligent in his work. Part of the time he sat in the room with me and was typing into his laptop computer. He had told me they went throughout the building asking different people to speak the planned sentences. It was the most real life testing I had ever experienced. I never knew what was going to be said or if it was a man or woman who would speak. In hearing tests, one usually repeats words such as "hot dog," "ice cream," "baseball." Over the years I began to learn the list of words and felt I was doing a good guessing job during hearing tests. I still believe this was true. I would watch the audiologist speak the words with her mouth covered with a piece of paper; yet if it was a two-syllable word, most of them would raise their shoulders slightly and drop again with each syllable. I was getting too good at reading body language.

While Tony sat behind me typing, a voice came on and I turned to Tony and said, "What did you say?" Then we laughed because I realized I had recognized his voice saying the test question. Later I recognized Dr. Dorman's voice and said so. Tony was surprised

I could distinguish voices, especially since I had only met Dr. Dorman for a few moments of conversation.

With my connections at ASU, months later a graduate student and research assistant, Susan Van Wie, asked me to help her test new sentences for standard hearing tests. I knew these tests needed improvement and I eagerly listened and repeated sentences for her research. My favorite sentence was, "Her smile was as smooth as creamed corn." It made me laugh at its originality and the fact I understood every word.

Her research proved popular and important as now they are called the AzBios and are being used at a small handful of clinics—notably Mayo Clinic, Rochester, according to Dr. Dorman. They are the subject of a recent paper from Mayo Clinic.[1]

Susan recently explained to me that the typical hearing tests used for testing people with potential hearing loss, like I described above, are too easy for CI patients and they get high scores up to 100%. The tests are called HINT sentences (Hearing in noise test) and CUNY (The City University of New York). "These tests can make it hard to evaluate progress with CI patients. That was a real issue for researchers and clinicians," Susan told me. "There was an interest in finding and developing more difficult sentences and thus (this became the catalyst for her thesis) the AzBios sentences were born." Susan said that Rene Gifford is a renowned researcher and apparently she liked her sentences well enough to publish the paper mentioned above. The sentences are spoken in an everyday conversational tone. Susan explained that the researchers are saying that the style is what is making them more difficult but she says, and I agree, that they are creatively written and that is another factor as to why they are more difficult. She wrote them with this in mind. As a patient,

---

1. "Speech Recognition Materials and Ceiling Effects: Consideration for Cochlear Implant Programs", R. Gifford, J. K. Shallop, and A. M. Peterson, *Audiology and Neurology*, 13, (2008): 193–205.

I agree with her and was excited I could understand her sentences. The laughter we shared that day still resonates in my mind, especially when I remember more of the sentences:

> Only the ant's coiled carcasses remain after the extermination.
> A camel is not the most comfortable animal on which to ride.
> The watermelon seed spitting contest ended in bitterness.
> Mom explained that rock salt was not for consumption.
> The baby ate a can of chili.
> He drank to excess after the hamster's death.
> They found a beak in the Thanksgiving turkey.
> We represent the lollypop guild.
> A six-foot skier falls harder than others.
> The incessant bird chirping became bothersome.
> The mindless chatter caused him to feel drowsy.

Thank you, Susan, for doing the in-depth research to help audiologists improve testing ability and for helping people with hearing loss be diagnosed more accurately. And most assuredly, thank you for the gift of laughter even in the throes of losing hearing or regaining that ability with a CI.

A few months after moving to the Southwest, I needed another mapping and contacted the Mayo Clinic. I met Louise Loiselle, cochlear implant specialist and she kept saying during the mapping, "You should not be able to hear this well." but I was. We joked that I could bluff like I did for many years.

About a year later, Louise asked if I would be a research subject for her doctorate research and I agreed. It was enjoyable and sometimes I, too, was amazed how easy it seemed to hear these sentences. After years of struggling to hear, this was fun and I would laugh often. I couldn't help it.

Louise told me that Tony at ASU wanted me to contact him to go in for more research testing but only using the ear level device: the newer invention that I didn't use as much as the body-worn device because the clarity was not the same when I first began wearing it. Later my Ohio audiologist, Laura Anderson, explained that had I begun wearing the ear level from the activation day, it would remain my preference. This made sense to me and I enjoy both devices equally today.

Tony also tested my ability to hear music played on the computer. I wasn't able to distinguish simple, familiar tunes and I was disappointed in the results, especially since I had spent so many years enjoying music. But he assured me it was fairly common that CI users were not enjoying music but that some were even able to pursue music as a vocation.

Some months later, a friend of mine, Jo Wrieden, was studying to become a speech therapist. She asked me to talk to her class about my CI experience. While waiting to talk, I read the American Speech-Language Hearing Association newspaper. One story told of how we hear music with our left ear, or right brain, and we hear speech with our right ear, or left brain.

It was a discovery that encouraged me to dig up my old hearing aids and put one in my left ear. I was amazed how well I could hear music pitches with the CI *and* the hearing aid. Some are beginning to have a CI in both ears. That may be in my future, but for now, this worked for me. I heard the words with my CI and the pitches fairly well with the hearing aid in my left ear. During my learning, I also found that it is easier to understand sentences than single words because we have context to figure out what is being said. Since this time, the hearing aid bit the dust and I am back to using only my CI.

Tony told me my ability to hear and understand was well above the median range of CI patients. Louise, at the Mayo Clinic, told me my ability to hear speech accurately in different settings was well above average. Although this thrills me, I don't stress this often because it could prove discouraging for other CI users whose ability is lower.

I never had this kind of testing prior to my implant, so I do not have an apples-to-apples comparison. I do have the testing from

January 8, 2002, which showed I was a candidate for a CI. When tested using 105 decibels of sound, I could discriminate zero words in my right ear and 8 percent in my left ear. On September 24, 2002, five months after my implant, at 55 decibels, I understood 96 percent. We can all agree my implant is successful.

Four Years Post Implant—Home Again

In November 2005, Bob and I decided we were homesick and wanted to move back to our home state, Ohio. We are diehard Buckeyes and didn't realize it until we heard the Ohio State University marching band play at a televised football game. I turned to Bob and said, "I want to go home." Our experiences moved with us. All the people we met and experiences we lived through will remain a part of our lives. We are blessed to have had the opportunity to live in the southwest and Pacific Northwest part of our country. We enjoyed the incredible beauty and fascinating people we met. But home is just that, home. Familiar with older memories and roots with family, friends and places.

In the time since my implant, I have never tired of sounds and continue to be tickled by new and much-loved sounds. It is like a nature walk on a new path each time I venture out into the world of sound. I hear different birds, music, voices, and more. When I meet someone for the first time, I no longer get the sick feeling in my gut that I won't understand his or her name. When the phone rings, I do check caller ID but no longer feel dread at picking up the receiver.

I continue to use closed captioning on the television because hearing is more relaxed for me in that atmosphere. When Bob or I are sick or we might be expecting visitors or phone calls, I sleep with my ear level device on. I learned to sleep with and without sounds.

My sign language is still intact. When I meet someone who uses ASL, I let them know mine is rusty but within a few minutes I am moving with ease. Although I know I am far from an expert, my goal to just communicate has stayed with me.

Looking Both Ways

During our lives we need to find time to travel on brief journeys into our past. I believe in living in the present, yet occasionally opening that old photo album showing where we have been can be therapeutic.

Working on this book is like opening my personal journal—which I have never kept. My columns ended up being my journal as I wrote about my past, present and future. Re-typing the columns, sometimes I found errors. But I also found that my thinking and coping with life's curves has evolved. Those times were often difficult and painful but I got through them—often with the help of friends and family.

When I became a copy desk typist at *SNP* and later a reporter, my mind opened like never before. When I first walked into *SNP* to meet Cliff Wilshire while I was still a guest columnist, I felt I had come to a place I knew years ago. Cliff asked me if I was disappointed in what I saw. I still remember my answer, "I had no expectations so I could not be disappointed."

Maybe that is how my life has been and will continue to be—no real expectations. Some may think that is setting the bar too low, but

I disagree. I think it is not setting the bar anywhere, thus allowing anything to happen, surprises and disappointments alike. I don't mean we should be careless, but I try not to have preconceived notions, and I walk into new experiences with a positive and open mind. Now my hearing has been restored, I can walk into a new adventure knowing I will at least understand what is happening around me. This feels like walking into a room filled with friends.

Butterfly Moments Can Come at Any Age

June 6, 2001

I know how a butterfly must feel when it first breaks out of its cocoon and spreads its wings. I must have been 8 or 9 years old when a monarch butterfly landed on my tennis shoe and slowly spread its wings, showing its vibrant colors. Fully expecting it to take flight, I held my breath. It stayed on my shoe. I remember looking around so I could find someone to share the moment with, but I was the sole witness of what I considered miraculous. I doubt the word miraculous popped into my young brain. More likely it was something like "special" or "Wow" that occurred to me.

So special was this moment that some 40 years later, I still can remember I was in the alley behind and between the Minors' and Bagleys' homes. Houses took on the name and personalities of the owners in old Westerville in the '50s. At least to me they did. I stood watching the butterfly, wondering what it meant that it stayed on my shoe so long. Did the butterfly like me? Had it chosen me? Remember, I was young. Time passed slowly on that hot summer day and I didn't move for fear the butterfly would take flight. Enjoying the company, I remember talking to it. People who know me realize it doesn't take much for me to begin talking.

Of course, eventually it did fly away and I pedaled my lavender and blue bicycle that my Dad had put together for me from old bike parts, home as fast as I could. I ran into our old house yelling for my mom, so I could share my butterfly experience with her. I think it was difficult for her to have to tell me that the butterfly had just freed itself from a cocoon, and it only had paused to dry its wings. But I knew it had chosen me to share its special moment of freedom.

Often we spend a lifetime binding ourselves into a self-made co-coon. I am not sure why this is often a human condition. We look, speak and act as society dictates, often losing our sense of self and thus losing true freedom. Thoughts occur to me at what might seem like odd times—in the car driving, in the shower and in dreams. Those all are times when I cannot act on the idea without great inconvenience.

While driving to interview a man running for public office, I had my butterfly moment. Thinking about my work, I understood how a butterfly must feel when it sheds its cocoon and spreads its wings while flying to freedom. It was a profound thought for me because I realized I felt that same freedom. I felt unbound and finally free to love life unabashedly and do what I love to do: meet people and write. "Wow!" entered my mind just as it had when that monarch butterfly landed on my shoe many years ago.

After that interview was complete, I dared share my new thought with this man I had just met. It seemed appropriate and inside I chuckled when his response was "Wow." He and I had talked about our shared goal of wanting to make a difference in this world. Our discussion was injected with a new energy when we talked about rep-resenting people honestly and well. Integrity. Values. Freedom. These are not new thoughts or ideas. But when you experience them in a way that reaches into your soul, it is all new and fresh. Everything I expe-rience has taken on a new vitality as if I had been partially asleep and now am awakened. I didn't realize how uninformed and uninvolved I had been prior to the last six months as a reporter.

I had no regrets and was thankful that as I turned a half century old, I could begin with an awareness that had been hidden as I was in my cocoon. Without the life experiences of the last 50 years, I most likely would never have shed that old cocoon, dried my wings and taken flight. Plus, with experience, fears of change and of learning are gone.

So I am running into my old house to share my news with you.

Reporting

The best part of reporting was meeting unique and diverse personal-ities. My husband, Bob, purchased what I called my "baby 'puter" with a fold-out keyboard so I could read lips and type while I interviewed people. It was really a hand-held computer but it was my baby and saved me a lot of time. I would go home and plug it into my home computer and send the text to work.

Every person has at least one story bursting to be told and I saw this easily. Sometimes it was newsworthy and often it was a story that just needed to be shared. When they were worth reporting, I relished working on those stories, sort of like I was fulfilling other people's desire to share something important to him or her.

Here are such people that I was either doing a story on or they were sources for stories.

Story Subjects Educate, Enlighten Me

April 17, 2002

Life has taught me to expect the unexpected, especially in my profession. My favorite part of reporting is meeting people, listening to their stories and writing about their lives. These times often are filled with surprises. The people I have interviewed have confirmed my belief that all of us are unique. Interviews and meetings have involved people of all ages in school, homes and municipal settings. Some were mourning a loss of a loved one, some were celebrating life and achievements, while others were voicing frustrations and potential solutions.

I feel honored to learn how people cope, dream and fulfill job obligations with a sense of pride. I stand in wonder at how people open up their hearts and minds for me to write about, yet others in public office who represent these same people often keep public issues private. It's a paradox I may never comprehend. I am encouraged there are more caring people in our communities than those wishing harm or secrecy. It is a wonder I am paid to do this job. I learn something new every day.

Recently I interviewed Upper Arlington's Super Senior of the Year, Dr. Harold "Doc" Edmondson. He and his wife, Caryl, made me feel welcome immediately. [Caryl died soon after this interview.]

Doc was sitting in a lawn chair out front waiting for me. He instantly smiled and waved when I pulled in the driveway. I knew I was at the right home meeting someone special. Doc said he was amazed to be selected as Super Senior for playing chess with children in the after-school program at Tremont Elementary School.

Doc does much more than play and teach chess. He also teaches children how to succeed and how to lose with a smile. "I want children to feel good about themselves," Doc said.

Does he ever "let them win"?

He replied with a question: "Let me ask you, you beat a child 20 times in a game, tell me how he likes it?"

He also teaches young people how to play shuffleboard at the UA Senior Center. Before his current lessons, Doc taught interpersonal communication at Capital University for 35 years. Each student must have brought home a feeling of accomplishment from his classes. Doc, now retired, kept turning our conversation to his wife and seven grown children. His youngest son, Joe, was at their home this day. Joe affirmed his dad's ability with children, talking about how much Doc had done for him, his siblings and friends throughout the years.

Doc said his memory isn't what it used to be, but he recited a poem freely for the story. "Some people say we only use about 30 percent of our brain, but Einstein said we don't use even 1 percent of our brain. So we can lose a lot of our brain power and still do well," Doc said. I think his mind is just fine. He remembers what is important.

The interview concluded, or so I thought. Doc had one more surprise in store. "We're not quite finished. Come on," said Doc heading for his back yard. You see, he also quizzed me during the interview and learned I had never played shuffleboard or chess.

I believe he opted for shuffleboard this day instead of chess because it was breezy and sunny. He guided me to his personal shuffleboard court, apologizing for the crack in the concrete. He placed something in my hands and said to toss it on the court.

"Those are tiny ball bearings," said Doc as I toss them and he hands me a stick to play. "My son, Bob, won a national shuffleboard tournament using that very stick," Doc said. I knew I was holding something very precious as Doc proceeded to teach me to play. With encouraging words such as, "hold it gently . . . that's it . . . good shot . . . try again," Doc showed me how to play.

I found I really liked the game but was undeserving of his final words to me. "It took me three years to learn this game, it would only take you three hours, Liz."

As I drove home, I found myself smiling. The child in me knew how the children at Tremont school must feel knowing Doc: successful, accepted and appreciated. He gives the children what he also gave me: a thirst to learn and his unhurried time. Thank you, Doc. I may never be a shuffleboard champ but I will think of you next time I play.

Chess anyone?

Doc was one of many fascinating people I met while I was a reporter. My communication skills of using body language always played an active role in understanding people I met. I was quick to let people know I was deaf without my hearing aids, and I would explain the best way to help me get the story—face me, talk naturally, move to a quiet room or area, don't shout and whatever I could think to help us talk easily.

People's Stories Make This Job Interesting
Winter 2001

Being a reporter is fun. "Fun? How could you say that?" you might ask. People make reporting an unexpected pleasure. Listening to other people's dreams, hopes, struggles and aspirations intrigues me and makes me want to improve my writing skills even more. Everyone has a story aching to be told, if someone would listen.

Meetings and agendas can be routine, but they're a necessary part of the job. Plus, I didn't know what a "plat" was until I attended a city council meeting. I now understand Robert's Rules of Order and I realize the magnitude of work it takes to manage a city or a school system while taking care to listen to individual needs.

The people I have met so far vary in age and interests. Some have won honors for work well done, some have worked wanting no honors or recognition, while others have overcome illness or are dedicated to finding causes and cures of illness. The list is infinite.

One day I met a man named Pudge. Pudge reminded me of my late father-in-law. After we were introduced, Pudge proceeded to chat and soon I realized he was an adept storyteller.

"Pudge, is that right? Pudge?" I asked. He smiled with his eyes. "You remind me of my father-in-law." Pudge's response was "Uh-oh, I'm in trouble now."

I assured him it was a compliment. Then I told him the man I called Dad also had been a person that told life stories while talking about his 80-plus years of life. I told him that Dad called me Lizziemae but I didn't know why.

"Why do they call you Pudge?" I asked, but I didn't quite get the answer. Still, I didn't feel like pressing him since we had just met. I wondered how I was able to understand Pudge so well, since he was working to speak because of some sort of tremor. But I could understand him and felt grateful for that small favor as we enjoyed our conversation.

I eventually learned what I had first suspected, Pudge's life holds many stories to be written and enjoyed, much the same as he enjoys life. As I said, he smiles with his eyes. You know people who smile with a hint of mischief hidden behind the squint of their eyes—a playful, kind mischief that amuses you and makes you want to know more. And I wanted to know more.

Pudge told me he is working with high school youth at the old schoolhouse at Fryer Park. A story to share, I just knew it. A few days later, we met to get this story and we went to the schoolhouse. It was blustery cold and wind whipped around us. I clicked a few photographs with my frozen fingers and looked around the old building. There was nothing but farmland all around us—nothing to block the wind and no windows in the schoolhouse.

Pudge told me that the weekend after Easter, there was going to be a Civil War re-enactment in the field near the schoolhouse. "You might want to do a story on that. There will be encampments, costumes and everything," Pudge said. I have found that people with one story usually know about many others. He pointed another direction and told me that the school children years ago were taken to a log cabin that was in the field ahead to eat lunch. Then they would come back to school.

His mother was one of those children, 100 years ago. Lou, a friend also working on the schoolhouse, was with Pudge that day and the three of us escaped to my car as I quickly warmed up the engine. As the warmth of the heat enclosed us, conversation warmed up as well. I proceeded with the interview and asked Pudge how long he had been married. He threw back his head, laughed heartily and said, "Oh, I have to get this right because it will be in the paper." He got it right; at least I haven't heard differently.

I did ask Pudge about the tremor in his voice and he took off his cap showing wavy, white hair and touched his scalp. He said that he has an implant under his scalp and in his chest to help control the tremor, at least on his right side. He held out his left hand and arm and it shook like when someone is shivering in the cold. I had not noticed that before (probably because we were all shivering) and at first thought he was joking with me. He wasn't.

Something about this man makes me think of the word perseverance, or determination. Pudge decided year's ago—maybe it was during World War II service or while helping raise his family or while working all these years—that life is worth living. He seems to understand that life hands us challenges that we can either greet and deal with or ignore and let them stifle us, not moving forward. Pudge obviously greets them and stands as an example for the upcoming generation.

Why do they call this Grove City man Pudge? That's another story waiting to be written, but be sure and ask when you meet him. Watch his smile as he tilts his cap and listen as history is told, the way it should be written in school books.

Life's lessons so far had been learned from remarkable people, and yes, of course some unremarkable people who taught me to persevere. But nature has always been the most special aspect in my life. Whether camping, hiking, sitting around a campfire, in the desert of Arizona or the rain of the Northwest, on a beach near an ocean or lake or in my own backyard, the beauty of nature never ceases to amaze and thrill me.

With nature, hearing is not necessary. Sure, hearing bird songs and the wind is wonderful but much of the outdoors is sights and scents.

Hope Floats When You're Doing Something You Love
December 27, 2000

I stepped outside into the wind of early winter and snow fell lightly. I exclaimed aloud, "The first snow!" and felt almost foolish. I just laughed and kept my face toward the falling snow. Smiling, I hoped I would never lose that childlike wonder of things like the first snow, Christmas morning, an old song. Watching the movie *Hope Floats* again, my favorite dialog was being spoken and I knew I must write about this. The main male character, Justin Matisse, is talking with his romantic counterpart, Birdee Pruitt.

He is a gifted craftsman and she is admiring the beautiful home that he designed and was building himself. Birdee asks why he goes around town painting houses when he could do so much more? Justin laughs, saying that she is talking about the American Dream, right?

Then he says, "I know what you mean. You start out loving something, you twist it and torture it trying to make money at it. You spend a lifetime doing that and at the end you can't find a trace of what you started out loving." He asks her what she started out loving and she can't remember. I thought about it. What did I start out loving in this life? Not able to answer my own question, I shifted my focus to my husband. An unfair tactic to keep from thinking, but I asked him what he started out loving. He said he would have to give it some thought. I anticipate a reply before the end of the year. I am not pressing him because his answer will be worth the wait.

Bob has a talent for saying the right thing at the right time. I agonized over a name for my column for some time. One evening I asked him, "Do you have any ideas for a name for my column? I am fresh out of creativity." He hesitated, maybe 30 seconds, and said, "How about 'Day by Day?'" I was stunned, not shocked but pleasantly wordless. "That's it," I replied with total satisfaction. Now my writing would involve Bob every time. He often helps when I am stuck with phrasing or meaning; he knows my personal goals and has always worked toward helping me achieve them.

As the blustery wind blew my hair today, I was not bothered. Then it hit me that I have always loved being outdoors and writing about it—in forest areas, near a lake or ocean, during any season but especially spring and autumn when the air is particularly fresh. I remember the first spring after one of my grandmothers died. I was sitting outside crying, thinking how she would have loved the day's weather: sunny, cool and a clear, blue sky. My mind was filled with memories of walking down her lane to get her mail while she would quietly sigh at a beautiful day, in no hurry. Is it genetic, this love of nature?

Our parents used to take us on Sunday drives after church. Westerville was small in those days and heading to the country was a drive of just a few minutes. We would come to a hill and at the top, it was almost inevitable for Dad to say, "Ohhhhhh look at that!" It might have been trees, a lake, a flock of birds, cows, sheep or any variety of nature's wonders spread before us. I don't think I appreciated it outwardly as a youngster but I remember agreeing privately that whatever it was, it was worth the ooooing and ahhhhing.

I started out loving the outdoors. Fresh air, sheets hung to dry outside that smelled like fresh air making sleep more restful, camping and sleeping in open fields under a moonlit sky, breathing the air that we are gifted to enjoy. At Girl Scout camp, everything smelled of canvas (usually wet) and wood. These memories are easily awakened with the familiar scents. When I was 13, our scouting unit slept at the edge of a wooded area on pine needles for mattresses. I remember waking and seeing two deer lying next to me. I moved and, naturally, they ran away. It seemed like a dream at the time, but the other girls saw the deer as well.

Maybe that is why I bought Save the Rain Forest coffee beans from the Arbor Day Web site. I sure didn't need another coffee mug, but it was a small way of saving what I love—nature in its purist, simplest form. As a child of the '50s, our entertainment was running, playing tag—yes, even what we called cigarette tag—skating, biking, mowing grass with push mowers (well, I remember it as entertainment) and swimming. At night we would wash our dirty, bare feet before climbing into bed with its fresh-air sheets awaiting us. There was no air-conditioning in homes, we slept with windows open and an old fan lulled us to sleep.

I started out loving pure nature. It is still a wonder to me, daily. As I recycle and use cloth napkins and rags, I hope to save a tree doing what I can to pass on some memories to the following generations.

What did you start out loving?

Keep Writing, Moving

The following poem was written during a long spell of sleeplessness. I could not sleep more than a few hours at night. (I would learn in 1998 that this was due to depression brought on by my MS. Medication has solved that issue.) This poem was written one very early morning—or late night, whichever way you see 2 A.M.—and I realized I was beginning to use my sleepless times more wisely, even though frustration was common.

Night Peace

December 2, 1997

Sometimes I lay awake at night
Wondering what to do,
Replaying the last day I spent,
Living the day through.
My mind does not want to rest;
I desire to with sleep be blessed.
Rather, lay awake I do.
Hours later, off I drift
To slumber, dreams anew;
Waking, hoping to feel at rest, and usually I do.
Is God attempting to stir my soul?
And I roll over and ignore?
When I lay awake at night
And arise to take pen in hand
The words that flow steadily from my heart
Often help me understand;
Pleased I listened to His gentle nudge,
Feeling blessed and full of love.
For I think God stirs us up
Makes us think and wakes us up,
Tossing and turning, wanting night peace.
If we submit our lives to God,
In the restless hours at night
He will stir our souls a bit.
So have a candle and keep it lit
And when we finally go to sleep
Angels will soothe us and rest will be deep.

Suweet-suwee-suweet!

I first heard this bird's song in Monroe, Washington, in 2005. Mornings, in particular, were quiet and wet with heavy dew making the grass slippery and shiny. Slug trails shimmered in the early morning light and spider webs were more visible with droplets of water decorating the delicate and lacey patterns. The air was fresh but cold enough to see my breath.

The pine trees soared toward the sky. The house we were living in was quite high in the mountains, where we were surrounded by three acres of yard, berry bushes, pine trees and various flora. The neighbors had a pony that seemed to waken when I let our dogs out. More than once, our golden retriever, Jack, took a statuesque stance staring down the brown and tan pony, possibly unsure what the creature was and how to approach it. The lure to run across the lane to meet him eye to eye was strong. I'm sure the pony was glad to be guarded by his fence and wood home.

But our dachshund, Snert, has never been shy and at first sight he dashed across the gravel lane and tried to work his way through the fence. Bravado is not always smart.

178

Our grandson Andrew and Pappy (Bob) ham it up.

It was on one of these mornings that I heard a new sound. It seemed distant but repeated every few seconds. I finally realized it was a bird I had never heard in my entire life and I was filled with awe and excitement. I'm not sure how long I listened but when I finally took the dogs inside, I opened the windows so I could hear the bird's song. Suweet-suwee-suweet—and each trill was about four or five pitches higher than the last. Now I wanted to learn the name of this sweet-sounding bird.

The neighbors I asked had not heard the bird and didn't know what it was by my rendition of its song. I went online searching for a site that shared bird songs but never did I find "my" bird. So I continued to enjoy the song and found myself often imitating it while I was doing housework or walking the dogs. Hopefully, no one but Bob heard me because he is used to my ways. It would be more than two years before I would hear the song again.

"Little Cabin, in the Woods . . ."

In May 2007, Bob and I met our daughter, Mary, her husband, Bob, and our three grandchildren, Jacob, Elizabeth and Andrew, in the Smoky Mountains outside Gatlinburg, Tennessee. We rented a cozy cabin called El Shaddai that offered, among other niceties, a big front porch with a swing, full-size rocking chairs and a remarkable view of the mountains. The cabin was perched rather high in the mountains and the green quiet did us all good for peaceful sleep and relaxation.

While the children lifted every rock looking for bugs, hiked up the hillside behind the cabin and swiftly slid down again, the adults did what we do well—rested on the porch while we knit, read, took pictures, talked and just savored the view.

The first morning, as I was on the porch watching the clouds rise around the mountains, I heard a range of birds singing and took the

Enjoying the Smokies.

sounds in with intense joy. Even though it has been five years since my cochlear implant, the sounds of nature still feel new and fresh each time I hear them again.

Then I heard it. "My bird" song—Suweet-suwee-suweet! I kept listening and smiling until someone else joined me and I asked them to listen. Soon everyone had heard it and no one knew the name of the bird. Since we were in the Smokies, there were sure to be rangers who might know. We stopped at the Sugarland's Visitor Center and I scooted right up to the information desk where four rangers were standing ready to help. I quickly asked about who might be able to tell me the name of the bird I kept hearing. I did my rendition of the bird's song and smiled. The four women chuckled and said my performance was really good but that the "birdman" wasn't in today.

"You might ask in the gift shop. They have a recording of bird songs," one woman said while pointing behind me.

"Thanks," I said turning to follow her instructions.

I asked one man if he had a recording of bird songs and I reenacted my version of the song. He held up his hand, and with a wry smile said, "Hold on. Follow me. We have sixty-seven songs on tape."

This man and another went to the back room with me on their heels. One man plugged in a CD to the overhead speaker and bird songs began loud and clear. It was rather exciting as I waited and listened to hear each song. No luck this day and I determined to come back. With my years of learning to cope with hearing loss, then deafness and also MS, I was no longer shy in my quest for answers.

Birdman of the Smokies

My one regret is I didn't get his name. This man who solved my two-year search shall remain nameless but important. I can see his slim, bespectacled, gray-bearded face and ready smile. But he was definitely the birdman of the Smokies.

I sang my bird's song to the best of my abilities and he smiled.

Bob and me with the grandchildren.

"I think I know who your bird is," he said as he pulled a book from under the counter. "Here it is. Lives at about 2,000 feet altitude and is rarely spotted but incredibly tame. The song is described as a slow trill of three pitches something like 'Look at me . . . way up here . . . higher, higher, higher.' "

"That's it! My bird," I exclaimed as he nodded and smiled. I thanked him for helping me end my book.

I'd been searching from April 2005 to this day, May 14, 2007 for the name of the bird whose song spoke to me. Now I know why: it's called the *Solitary Vireo*. How alone I had felt in my deafness and when sound returned, I might as well have been that Vireo saying, "Here I am . . . way up here . . . higher, higher, higher!"

The description in the *National Audubon Society Field Guide to North American Birds* even sounds a bit like me in behavior.

". . . It is extraordinarily tame and seems to ignore humans near its nest; frequently an incubating bird will allow itself to be touched. Like other Vireos, it moves slowly and deliberately through the trees, peering with head cocked to one side in search of insects."

I think I am quite tame, and though I never ignored humans, I was accused of this on account of my hearing loss; I move slowly and deliberately—but not through trees—due to MS; and am known to cock my head to one side to hear better but, please, no insects.

Since this adventure, I have been told the solitary vireo has been re-named the *blue headed vireo*. But I continue to think of her as my solitary vireo. I may never see that Vireo but I know her well.

Thanks for listening, friends.

Appendix
Technical Description of Cochlear Implant Mapping

By Paula Dendiu Beale, M.A., CCC-A

First we connect the patient's speech processor to the programming computer by means of a cable that is connected to the base (usually, depending on the processor) of the processor. We place the processor and coil on the patient's head, and then, depending on the style of implant that the patient has, we have the option to do a couple of different things. The older generation of implant (Nucleus 22) requires us to check the thickness of the skin flap over the internal device. We do this by means of a test that we run using the programming computer, while the patient is wearing the coil and processor. The Nucleus 24 and Freedom internal devices have a function that is called telemetry, which is defined by Cochlear Corporation as "the ability to read back diagnostic information sent by the implant about its functionality." We can "test the implant," to get a measure of the impedance levels of the implanted electrodes, to be sure that all of the electrodes are functioning properly. During this test, the patient usually hears or feels nothing, as the electrical stimulus used to test the electrodes is typically lower than the patient can perceive.

Next, we tell the patient that we will be playing a series of beeps. The patient is instructed to listen, and to tell us as soon as he hears or feels anything, as the patient may not only hear, but also, (or only), feel the stimulation. We want to know the softest sound that the patient perceives, so we will stimulate until the patient responds, then go back to a lower stimulation level, and stimulate again until the patient responds again. When we arrive at a loudness level where the patient responds consistently at least a couple of times, that is the level that we call the patient's "threshold," or the softest sound that the patient can recognize. This becomes the "T-level" of the patient's MAP. In order to reach a consistent response from the patient, and to know that the patient isn't signaling when there is no stimulus, some audiologists will present a series of soft sounds, and ask the patient to count the number of beeps that she hears. That way, the audiologist knows that the patient truly heard the sounds, since she correctly identified the number of beeps presented. We determine the T-levels for anywhere from five to all twenty-two of the electrodes to create the MAP. This is because we can measure as few as five electrodes, and then "interpolate," or ask the computer to fill in the T-levels for the remaining electrodes, based on an algorithm built into the program.

When we have completed the threshold levels, we move to the Comfort levels. We ask the patient to listen to a series of beeps which will gradually become louder. The patient is instructed to follow along with a loudness chart, which identifies sounds as T-level, Soft, Medium, Loud but Comfortable (C-level) and TOO LOUD. We ask that the patient let us know when the loudness of the sound reaches a point where the beeps sound loud, but comfortable, a level that the patient feels is the loudest level that she can tolerate for long periods of time. Setting these levels at an appropriate level will ensure that the sounds in the patient's environment will never be uncomfortably loud. The combination of these two measures, T-level and C-level, determines the dynamic range of electrical stimulation for each electrode pair.

Next, we ask the patient to listen to a series of beeps, which may be presented in groups of five, ten, or more electrodes, and at one or two loudness levels. We ask the patient to let us know if any of the electrodes sound louder or softer than any of the others. This is known as "sweeping" the electrodes. This helps us to make a MAP that sounds smooth and even in loudness to the patient.

Then, we "balance" the electrodes. This involves asking the patient to listen to beeps from two different electrodes (usually adjacent), which are presented to the patient in an alternating manner, usually at medium or loud levels. We ask the patient to try to ignore the pitch differences and let us know if one sound is louder or softer than the other. Again, this just helps us to refine the MAP for the patient, since the MAP typically sounds best to the patient when all electrodes sound as similar in loudness as possible.

Finally, we "Go live." We turn on the processor and ask the patient to listen to voices, and to evaluate the loudness and quality of the sounds the patient is hearing. We typically begin speaking at a soft level, especially at the first few mapping sessions, and gradually turn up the loudness for the patient as we talk. Then, we can make adjustments based on the patient's perception of the sounds she is hearing. For example, we can alter the "Gain" of the sound, which allows us to selectively increase or decrease the low-pitched or high-pitched sounds presented to the patient, in the event that voices sound too low- or high-pitched. We can also make many other adjustments to the MAP at this time, to optimize the patient's perception of speech.

For patients using the Freedom or Sprint speech processors, we can next add the SmartSound options, such as ADRO, Beam,

Whisper or Autosensitivity, or a combination of these to the basic MAP, to allow the patient to modify the sounds she hears in different environments.

For some patients, especially at the initial MAPping sessions, we will only measure T-levels on five specific electrodes. Then we immediately "Go live" with speech at a very soft level, and gradually increase the loudness until it sounds comfortable for the patient. This is an easy way to get sound to a patient quickly, especially if the patient is having trouble identifying appropriate levels during the initial sessions. As time progresses, and the patient becomes a more sophisticated listener, more specific T- and C-levels can be measured for each electrode in order to optimize the patient's MAP.

Once the maps are made, we try to assess the patient's speech understanding, using some basic listening tasks. Often, at least at the initial session, we will walk the patient around the office to expose him to a variety of new sounds, and to be sure that no environmental sounds are uncomfortable for the patient. We will also at times work with the patient on auditory rehabilitation tasks, demonstrating to the patient and family how best to practice listening at home.

So, that is MAPping, in a (very large) nutshell.

Paula Dendiu Beale, M.A., CCC-A
Audiologist
Ohio ENT

Lightning Source UK Ltd.
Milton Keynes UK
UKOW05f0115120214

226289UK00002B/61/P